The Almoravid Maghrib

PAST IMPERFECT

See further
www.arc-humanities.org/our-series/pi

The Almoravid Maghrib

Camilo Gómez-Rivas

British Library Cataloguing in Publication Data
A catalogue record for this book is available from the British Library

ISBN (print) 9781641890854
e-ISBN (PDF) 9781802701432
e-ISBN (EPUB) 9781802701449

www.arc-humanities.org
Printed and bound in the UK (by CPI Group [UK] Ltd), USA (by Bookmasters), and elsewhere using print-on-demand technology.

Contents

List of Illustrations

*for Zélie, and in memory of her grand-
dads, Alberto and Michel, who would have
enjoyed reading this book*

Acknowledgements

This work was made possible by generous funding from the Alexander von Humboldt Foundation in Germany, where I spent two years in residence and mapped out this book. Special thanks to my academic host at the Center for Near and Middle Eastern Studies at Philipps-Universität Marburg, Albrecht Fuess. Final writing and revision was made possible by two quarters without teaching in the Department of Literature at the University of California, Santa Cruz. I would like to thank the in-house editor at Arc Humanities Press who gave excellent editorial and stylistic guidance as well as to the peer reviewer whose comments were particularly insightful. I have done my best to incorporate their valuable suggestions. Thanks to my departmental colleagues Sharon Kinoshita, for her mentorship and guidance, and to Filippo Gianferrari. Both read the manuscript, made valuable suggestions, and helped me work out central ideas. Most special thanks to Emmanuelle, for her support and partnership, for reading the manuscript and talking me through the many compositional decisions.

Abbreviations and Note on Language and Dates

Certain symbols, or diacritical markings, are used to render Arabic in English or the Arabic alphabet with the Latin one. Lines over vowels denote long vowels and dots under consonants denote emphatic consonants. Most of these markings have been dispensed with here, however, retaining only the *hamza* (') and *'ayn* (') in names and toponyms. Bibliographical notes and foreign words in italics are the exception and are rendered with full transliteration. Those who don't know Arabic can ignore these symbols and read as if they were not there. Words that have entered English usage, according the New Oxford American Dictionary, are neither italicized nor fully transliterated (e.g., hadith, imam, qadi, Qur'an). Names and place names come from several languages (Berber/Amazigh, Arabic, Castilian) and their English usage has been affected by different historical regimes, including French and Spanish colonial projects. Common usage, again according to the dictionary, has been used to determine which form to use (e.g., Marrakesh over Marrakush or Marrakech), although some of the decisions are certainly subjective and imperfect. I would have preferred Sabta over Ceuta, but I feel readers will recognize the latter more easily.

The Islamic calendar, known as the Hijri calendar, begins in the year 622 CE. As a lunar calendar, the year is about eleven days shorter than the solar one. To reflect the Arab-Islamic sources and chronology and the different senses of historical time in our period, both Hijri and Gregorian (Common Era) dates are kept, divided by a slash: Hijri/CE. Events recorded on specific dates include Islamic day and month names.

Many Arabic masculine names include the term *ibn*, which is shortened here to "b." unless appearing at the beginning of the name.

Sources or works that are listed in the Further Reading are only given in their shortened form (e.g., author and short title) in the footnotes. The following two reference works employ an abbreviation:

EI2   *Encyclopedia of Islam*, 2nd ed., edited by P. Bearman, Th. Bianquis, C. E. Bosworth, E. van Donzel, and W. P. Heinrichs (Leiden: Brill, referenceworks.brillonline.com).

EI3   *Encyclopedia of Islam*, 3rd ed., edited by Kate Fleet, Gudrun Krämer, Denis Matringe, John Nawas and Everett Rowson (Leiden: Brill, referenceworks.brillonline.com).

Principal Characters
in the Narrative

In order of appearance:

Yahya b. Ibrahim	Guddala chief who first recruits Ibn Yasin on return from hajj
Waggag b. Zalwi	Ibn Yasin's teacher
'Abd Allah b. Yasin (Ibn Yasin)	Founder of Almoravids
Yahya b. 'Umar	Lamtuna chief, first Almoravid amir
Abu Bakr b. 'Umar	Second Almoravid amir
Yusuf b. Tashfin	Third Almoravid amir; Abu Bakr's cousin
Zaynab al-Nafzawiyya	Queen of Aghmat; marries Abu Bakr
'Abd Allah b. Buluggin	Last Zirid amir of Granada
al-Mu'tamid b. 'Abbad	Last ruler of Taïfa of Seville
Sir b. Abi Bakr	Nephew and one of the ablest commanders of Yusuf
'Ali b. Yusuf b. Tashfin	Yusuf's son and fourth Almoravid amir
Ibn Rushd al-Jadd	Important jurist from Córdoba
Muhammad b. Tumart (Ibn Tumart)	Founder of Almohad movement
Tamim b. Yusuf	Half brother of 'Ali; important Almoravid commander and governor

Tashfin b. ʿAli	ʿAli's son and last capable military leader of Almoravids
ʿIyad b. Musa	Important jurist and last Almoravid leader of Ceuta
Banu Ghaniya	Almoravid governors and their successors who survived into the Almohad period as rebel leaders

Introduction

The emergence of the Almoravid Empire in northwestern Africa signalled a turning point. For this region known as the Far Maghrib (*al-Maghrib al-Aqṣā*), the appearance of this powerful religious and political movement was linked to profound social, economic, and political changes that transformed the life of the region's diverse communities. Plainly put, the Almoravids (Arabic *al-Murābiṭūn*) introduced state structures of a quality and scale that were entirely unprecedented in the region. They brought about the first political and administrative unification of the Far Maghrib and Western Sahara, a region that today comprises Morocco and much of Algeria and Mauritania, under an indigenous, Berber leadership. This new state, also unprecedentedly, annexed al-Andalus (or Muslim Iberia), constituting the first Maghribi conquest of al-Andalus, and the first unification of the two regions since the Syrian Umayyad conquest of the second/eighth century. (The Syrian Umayyads of Damascus were the early Islamic Caliphate that conquered much of the Iberian Peninsula and North Africa, or the Maghrib, in the second century of the Islamic calendar). This large scale administrative unification was brought about by the creation of a new literate class. As a result, a series of new institutions took shape in the Maghrib, affecting military organization, bureaucratic practice, legal, urban, and commercial life. The initial emergence of the movement was brought about by the formation of a tribal confederation of redoubtable military ability. Later, military forms and institutions were implemented along models existing in the Islamic East (the *Mashriq*). A bureaucratic elite, including legal practitioners, evolved significantly and involved the creation of new educational arrangements and practices. New cities appeared, chief of which was Marrakesh, the Almoravid capital. But the existing urban centres were also transformed decisively, such as was the case with Fes, Tlemcen, Sijilmasa, and Ceuta. This urban development provides the best evidence of a sharp rise in economic activity, including agriculture and manufacture, but also long distance commercial trade, a practice amply in evidence as a signature trade of the Almoravids. This entailed the introduction of a gold currency that became widely disseminated and the promotion of trans-Saharan and Mediterranean commerce on a new level, using novel legal and commercial instruments. All of this was accompanied by the articulation of a new kind of state legitimacy and a new kind of religious life.

The scope and full detail of the transformation involved in the rise of the Almoravid Maghrib is still poorly understood, especially in English language scholarship, which has long neglected the Maghrib and its history. For a long time, the history of the Almoravids was framed in very simplistic terms, as the rise of a religious, mostly fanatical, movement, giving little to no attention to the nuanced social and economic aspects of their emergence. Historians writing in English had focused their efforts and interests on al-Andalus and its significance to European history and on the Eastern Islamic World, home of the central and foundational forms and narratives of Islamic history. This is related to, and compounded by, an abiding interest in the formation of classical Islamic civilization at the expense of post-classical Muslim cultures and histories. This has led to superficial readings of episodes, such as that of the Almoravids, who have been portrayed as unfortunate interlopers into Andalusi history and its European stage, or as entirely peripheral to Islamic history. Both geographically and temporally, it was thought to have occurred during a period of time after which Islamic civilization had supposedly reached its apex and ceased being creative and original. In many ways, the opposite is true: the Islamic forms that survived into later history were thoroughly transformed in this post-classical period, and neglect of the latter has caused a series of distortions and misinterpretations.

Fortunately, historiographical traditions in other languages have not been as neglectful. Arabic historiography from the Maghrib, both old and new, has an entirely different level of commitment to the subject. Spanish and French, for different reasons, including imperial and colonial interests, present nuanced and sustained approaches. And English language scholarship of the last decade has turned a corner and dedicated more continuing and quality attention to the Almoravid Maghrib, with the appearance of the first monographs and comprehensive histories written in English on the subject. This book is the result of this change in attitude and interest. *The Almoravid Maghrib* argues that far from being a simple zealous or fanatical religious movement, the Almoravids brought about a transformative episode of state formation, which proved foundational for several of the region's social and political traditions. This transformation did involve the introduction of a new and widely influential religious culture, but it did not stop at that, nor was the religious dimension the most impactful in the long run. The religious transformation of the Far Maghrib under the Almoravids coincided with an economic and social revolution, several of the effects of which were of abiding influence, such as the centrality of the new capital city or the prominence of the legal tradition they sponsored. Far from being just a militaristic religious movement, this book argues that the Almoravids implemented new practices that served key purposes, including commercial legislation and arbitration, legal and urban administration and political legitimation, diplomacy, and international relations.

This is not to say that the Almoravids were not a religious movement. They cultivated a fierce piety that was in many ways intolerant, if not always against Christians and Jews, which, I will argue, they were less so than their successors, pointing to a broader regional evolution, beyond the specifics of Almoravid theology, then certainly against Kharijis, Baja-liyya Shi'a, and other forms of "heterodox" Islam, which they made their central mission to eradicate. The Almoravids cultivated a concrete theology and praxis that transformed religious practice and Muslim identification in the Far Maghrib. This dimension was so powerful that it awakened both a passionate following and forms of resistance and opposition, which took on their own surprising and novel spiritual and religious expressions. One of these would eventually overwhelm the new state. The Almoravids revolutionized the political and economic structures of the Far Maghrib. They also awakened powerful and creative spiritual and religious energies and expressions. These are deeply interrelated developments, with no direct or clearly traceable causality.

This book unpacks the elements of this argument and the separate dimensions of the transformation of the Almoravid Maghrib over six chapters, which are chronologically ordered, and, to some extent, narratively arranged. Each chapter begins with a narrative description involving an important historical character from Almoravid history. This mode of presentation has two goals in mind: the first is to give the reader stories and characters to relate to, because, to some extent (even if sometimes very limited), these stories and the lives they represent provide a window onto an experience of an era only dimly perceived from our vantage and therefore sometimes best grasped through story and character. The second is to underline something that may seem the opposite of the first, which is that the stories themselves, which are often, if not always legendary or fictive, are cultural products, in and of themselves, of the era and of its ensuing reception and transmission. They provide a kind of literary map to how the historical experience was remembered and made sense of by later generations. The biographies and narratives, which are part of a complex layered literary tradition, are worth knowing as such, as literary products of the Maghribi and Arabic historiographical imaginary. This tension (between historical and literary, between real and fictive) is something readers of medieval history can benefit from keeping in mind.

Each narrative description is followed by, or gradually gives way to, a discussion of the aspects of Almoravid history most relevant to it, through chronological or thematic correspondence. Chapter 1 features the first leader of the Almoravids and the social context out of which this spiritual founder emerged. Chapter 2 begins with a description of a queen figure form the region of Marrakesh, who the Almoravid leadership co-opted through the traditional means of political marriage, and depended upon for further expansion. Chapter 3 begins with the experience of one of the Muslim kings deposed by the Almoravids in al-Andalus, leading into a discussion of the meaning of the Andalusi experiment for the Almoravid Maghrib. Chapter 4 takes stock of the transformation of the Almoravid Maghrib by its mid-point, opening with a description of the second longest serving Almoravid amir (ruler, commander). Chapter 5 opens with the lives of two oppositional religious figures who rose to challenge Almoravid politics and theology. And Chapter 6 tells of two loyalists, one who held out to the very end, and who survived and was succeeded by rebels who championed their Almoravid identity for a surprisingly long time, leading to a discussion of the afterlife of the Almoravids and their long term influence in the region.

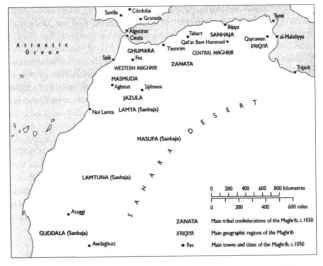

Figure 1: The distribution of the Berber peoples, ca. 1050, adapted from Amira K. Bennison, *The Almoravid and Almohad Empires* (Edinburgh: Edinburgh University Press, 2016), 25. Reproduced with permission of the Licensor through PLSclear.

Chapter I

The Preacher

The rise of the Almoravids can appear as an accident of history, its founding figure mysteriously emerging from the very margins of the known Muslim world, when, in fact, he was part of a longer process of Islamization of the southern Maghrib, the Sahara, and the Sahel, which gradually engaged with dimensions of religious, political, and economic life, at least until his emergence, which can be read as a punctuated episode of rapid development after a gradual build-up.

Ibn Yasin's Youth

When he was old enough to travel, ʿAbd Allah b. Yasin left his village of Tamamanawt, on the southern edges of the desert, to join a teacher who lived over the mountains in the valley of the Sus.[1] He was sent off with a caravan on the month-long

---

1 Abū ʿUbayd al-Bakrī, *Kitāb al-Masālik wa'l-Mamālik* (Beirut: Dār al-Gharb al-Islamī, 1992), 859; *Corpus of Early Arabic Sources*, ed. Levtzion and Hopkins, 71; Bosch Vilá, *Almorávides*, 51. Little is known about the early life ʿAbd Allah b. Yasin, and the available information is contradictory. Al-Bakri's geographical work gives us the precious detail of the name of his mother's village. I am imagining Ibn Yasin leaving from his mother's village to join Waggag; but he may have moved to other villages of the region in his youth. According to one tradition (*al-Ḥulal al-Mawshiyya*) he spent seven years studying in al-Andalus before returning to "the

journey to where this teacher of growing regional reputation, Waggag b. Zalwi, had established a school or religious settlement (a *ribāṭ* known as the *Dār al-Murabiṭīn*).[2] Ibn Yasin's family connections in the Sus would make sure he was properly set up and arrange for news to get back by means of the traders who regularly came through; his mother and father, Tin Izamaren and Yasin, had relations who travelled and traded with towns across the great desert and in the valleys of the Sus, the Draʿa, and the Tafilalt, where the caravan city of Sijilmasa was located. Ibn Yasin and his family stood to gain considerable benefit if he developed his aptitude for letters and piety in the way of the faith, which had grown steadily over the years in the village (where some of the old ways still held). Ibn Yasin would go to the *Dār al-Murābiṭīn* to learn the path of true knowledge and the true religion from shaykh Waggag, and perhaps he would bring some of this knowledge back to teach the others. The journey was long and difficult, and the people and their customs seemed strange to young Ibn Yasin, unlike what he had known in his home in the south. In the Sus, a valley protected by rocky foothills on the northern edges of the Sahara, where sand

---

Far West." Bosch Vilá thinks this unlikely and I would concur. *Corpus of Early Arabic Sources*, ed. Levtzion and Hopkins, 313. My opening is therefore slightly speculative. Al-Bakri placed Tamamanawt or Temamenaout on the edge of "the Sahara of the city of Ghana," implying a southern location, although the French geographer Capitaine Monteil identified it with Tamanart in the Draʿa, on the northern border of the Sahara, in Morocco. It should be noted also that Saharan edges or borders move and shouldn't be understood or conceived as sharp or concrete, but as gradual border areas that have moved and changed over the centuries. There is nothing to indicate that the area was substantially greener in the mid-fourth/tenth, when our narrative begins, and yet there has been an ongoing process of desertification.

2 "Religious settlement" is Bennison's formulation. Bennison, *Almoravid and Almohad Empires*, 27. On the evolution of the meaning of *ribāṭ*, see Meier, "Almoravids and Marabouts." Also, J. Chabbi and Nasser Rabbat, "Ribāṭ," EI2.

and stone give way to greener valleys that climb into the snow-capped mountains of the High Atlas, people spoke and dressed differently. But Ibn Yasin would adapt and learn and come to know of places, even further east and north, where students pursued the same path. This network of pious students and scholars formed a kind of far-flung brotherhood of those devoted to the faith, through reading and contemplation, striving to understand the scripture, which was explained and debated by generations of the learned and pious who had transmitted the divine message all the way from Muhammad in Medina over the four centuries since the revelation.[3] Ibn Yasin hoped to emulate these pious scholars, to achieve a basic education in their texts and genres, starting with the Qur'an and the traditions of the sayings and actions of the Prophet and those of his companions.

And Ibn Yasin did thrive. He applied himself assiduously to learn and master the opinions and interpretations of the scholars before him, in the tradition taught by his teacher. The earliest amongst the teachers of this particular scholarly tradition, Malik b. Anas of Medina (d. 179/795), had lived in the city in Arabia where Muhammad had founded his first community of believers, committed to following the path shown by God through His divine revelation in the Qur'an. Malik b. Anas learned and recorded what Muhammad said and did from a generation that had known him personally. He had also recorded how the Prophet's earliest community of faith in Medina had lived according to the example he set, meeting and negotiating the challenges that all communities encounter. Malik recorded all of this into what became the first, or earliest, extant collection of hadith (the sayings and actions of Muhammad), known as *Kitāb al-Muwaṭṭa'* (The Book of the Well-Trodden Path), which he taught to a generation of students, including some of the greatest scholars of the Muslim tradition (Imam al-Shafi'i, the eponymous founder of

---

3 When, according to Muslim tradition, the archangel Gabriel revealed the text of the Qur'an to Muhammad over a period of twenty-three years, between 610 and 633.

the Shafiʿi School is perhaps the best known).[4] Two hundred and forty years after Malik's death and six thousand kilometres (four thousand miles) away in the Far Maghrib, Ibn Yasin's teacher cultivated this same scholarly faith tradition, known as the Maliki *Madhhab* or School of Malik, which was taking root in the southwestern desert, at the outer limits of the Muslim network of communities, along with the Muslim way of life of which it was an integral part. We can imagine this network as one giant land mass, but the reality was more diffuse and diverse and intermingled with non-Muslim communities. Ibn Yasin joined this network as a cultural outsider from a borderland culture (seen from the perspective of the Muslim cultural heartland). He spoke a different language and hailed from a cultural tradition altogether different from those which had dominated the classical traditions of Islam, most closely associated with the Arabic and Persian languages, and the traditions of Syria, Iraq, Arabia, and Egypt. Ibn Yasin's village and the pastoralist communities around it in Mauritania and the Western Sahara spoke a variety of Berber or Amazigh, an umbrella term for the indigenous language, people, and culture of the Maghrib and had only recently begun the process of conversion to Islam (through religious conversion and cultural contact and integration). In the years studying under Waggag, Ibn Yasin became adept at these Arab-Islamic traditions, while retaining fluency in his own language, tradition, and customs. He was deeply pious and had earned a reputation as an outstanding and dedicated student. So when a Maliki scholar leading a party to the western Sahara from

---

4 Muhammad b. Idris al-Shafiʿ (d. 204/820), eponym of the Shafiʾi *madhhab* (school of Islamic Law), was a student of Malik, eponym of the Maliki School. They are two of what became known as the four schools of Sunni Law or *madhhabs*. The other two are the Hanafi and Hanbali Schools. Their evolution and identification as central components of Sunni Islam was a gradual process, only fully consolidating in the third and fourth centuries of Islam. The most recent translation of Malik's *Muwaṭṭaʾ* is: Mālik b. Anas, *al-Muwaṭṭaʾ, the Royal Moroccan Edition*.

across North Africa approached Waggag, stating that he was seeking a volunteer to lead a mission into the western desert, someone possessing deep knowledge of the faith in order to teach the people of the south the true ways and traditions, Waggag did not hesitate. He recommended Ibn Yasin on the basis of his knowledge, his piety, and his leadership.

The party making its way to the western desert included members returning from pilgrimage to distant Mecca (a journey of many months). The most prominent among these was Yahya b. Ibrahim, chief of the Berber Sanhaja tribe of the Guddala of the western desert. The other was the Maliki scholar who approached Waggag. His name was Jawhar b. Sakkum. Versions of this story differ (concerning who was in the party and who they spoke to), but it is said that on their stop-over in Qayrawan,[5] Yahya communicated his desire to a leading scholar there, Abu 'Imran al-Fasi (d. 430/1039), to find a teacher to bring back to the Guddala to impart knowledge of the faith among his people who knew little beyond the rudiments of belief. Faith in Islam had been growing among the tribes and villages of the southern Maghrib and across the great desert. The Guddala chief and his shaykh wanted a dedicated teacher to afford greater guidance in learning the way of true belief. It is likely that they had also wanted to cement their relationship with this great city and its wealth of connections to the east and bring home a tangible representative of that connection. But as it turned out, no scholar in Qayrawan was willing to undertake the arduous journey or was deemed by Abu 'Imran to have had the requisite characteristics, presumably including good knowledge of the language and cultural practices of the Sanhaja (the wider tribal affiliation to which the Guddala belonged) as well as thorough grounding in Islamic texts and practices. He directed them instead to Waggag, who operated much closer to their destination and had better ties to the region. Waggag in turn would recommend one of his star students, 'Abd Allah b. Yasin, who

---

5 From where Islam and the Maliki traditions had first come west, some 2500 km (1500 miles) away.

was a Sanhaja Berber of the Gazula tribe, a neighbour of the Guddala in the western Sahara. Ibn Yasin thus joined Yahya and Jawhar's party for the last leg of their journey, travelling through a network of resting places and watering holes, deep into the western desert. There, under the aegis of chief Yahya b. Ibrahim, Ibn Yasin began his mission, preaching and teaching among the Guddala, leading the community in belief and prayer as their new imam.

Early Failure and Growth

Ibn Yasin had much to learn. This became painfully evident when his patron, Yahya b. Ibhrahim, died unexpectedly and a number of the Guddala (including Jawhar) expressed their unhappiness with Ibn Yasin's spiritual leadership, especially his strict application of moral discipline. They hounded him out of the village. In what was perhaps his greatest personal crisis, Ibn Yasin fled the immediate region and was compelled to reconsider his entire mission and where he'd gone wrong in pursuing his vision of shaping a righteous community. Versions of what happened next differ. In the more legendary version, Ibn Yasin and a circle of his closest supporters took refuge in an island hideout where they built a sanctuary for spiritual devotion, another *ribāṭ* (a religious settlement, traditionally believed to have been located off the coast of Mauritania).[6] From here they began their righteous struggle against the recalcitrant Guddala, strengthened by a new-found clarity of purpose, an image reinforced by the narrative's echo of the Prophetic *sīra* (Muhammad's biography or hagiography), specifically the episode when the Quraysh had turned against Muhammad and forced him and his closest circle to flee after a period of harassment and beatings, to found a new community of belief (in Medina). Ibn Yasin would also found a new community of belief in the image of that earliest of the community of believers, after weathering the dark

---

6 The classic article on investigating its location is Moraes Farias, "The Almoravids."

moment of personal crisis and peril. Conveniently (perhaps too much so) the story provides an origin for the name by which Ibn Yasin's movement came to be known: the Almoravids (from the Arabic *murābiṭ*: dweller of a *ribāṭ*; but, more precisely, a pious devotee, dedicated to the path of God, a related concept).

Earlier and more credible sources lend credence to a more prosaic version. Expelled by the Guddala, Ibn Yasin appears to have returned to his former teacher at the *Dār al-Murābiṭīn* in the Sus. Waggag comforted and counselled Ibn Yasin and convinced him after some time to return to his mission. Waggag exercised his influence for Ibn Yasin to be allowed to return with the desert Sanhaja, this time with a new patron who was a chief of a neighbouring tribe (confusingly also named Yahya). Yahya b. ʿUmar was chief of the Lamtuna Sanhaja; his mother, Safiyya, appears to have been the sister of Ibn Yasin's first patron, Yahya b. Ibrahim. Ibn Yasin had thus withdrawn for a time and returned bolstered by Waggag's counsel to forge a new relationship and a new beginning with a different branch of the desert Sanhaja. Members of this branch, of the Sanhaja Lamtuna, were eager to benefit from the spiritual guidance for which Ibn Yasin had begun to become known, as well as from benefits associated with establishing connections to the wider world of learning represented by Maliki scholars like Ibn Yasin and Waggag. Chastened by his experience, Ibn Yasin applied himself to his mission with renewed fervour, preaching, praying, and teaching among the Lamtuna.

In this new arrangement with the Lamtuna, and under the aegis of Yahya b. ʿUmar, a movement took shape. Ibn Yasin's spiritual stature grew as the movement gradually consolidated into a confederation of tribes propelled by a powerful new religious identity and ideology. Increasingly, their energy would be directed outward, turning from an internal struggle to one directed to convert and reform those around and beyond them. The first struggle and subjugation was against the rebellious Guddala (Ibn Yasin's first hosts). This formative—one might say the foundational or model—experience provided a template for further expansion as a federation (an alliance of local clans and tribes) emerged with a clearer spiritual mission, complemented by a military ability. Ibn Yasin's mission thus evolved from instruction, teaching, and preaching, to a more confrontational encounter with neighbouring communities deemed pagan or heretical. Ibn Yasin combined spiritual, political, and military leadership, leading his followers into battle and assuming the role of charismatic leader, which also involved entering into a series of marriages—likely as part of forging the federation of western Saharan tribes. The image that emerges of his style of leadership from the earliest sources (none of which witnessed him personally) is a contradictory one, contradictions which stem from the perspectives and identity of authors of these sources.

One valuable early source by a near contemporary Andalusi geographer, Abu 'Ubayd al-Bakri (d. 487/1094), portrays Ibn Yasin as a coarse fanatic, whose methods were informed, ultimately, by what al-Bakri interpreted as ignorance of the basic tenets of Islam and of important details of theology and law. Al-Bakri closes his uncharitable description of the founder of the Almoravids with a list of eccentricities and mistakes perpetrated by the rustic and eccentric preacher and his followers in the name of the faith. Examples included inflicting whippings on new adepts for past sins and for skipping ablutions.[7] Al-Bakri's description reads like a warning and illustration of the dark turn the ignorant (and culturally other) can give to what was a sophisticated religious and intellectual tradition in a civilized environment (such as al-Bakri's own Andalusi milieu). A second early source, by 'Iyad b. Musa (known as Qadi 'Iyad d. 544/1149; see Chapter 6), writing a generation later and from the Mediterranean coast of Morocco, presents a diametrically opposite picture. For 'Iyad, an accomplished scholar and jurist, Ibn Yasin was a paragon of learning, piety, and courage, combined into an exemplary personality and heroic historical founding figure. 'Iyad writes that Ibn Yasin's

---

7 Al-Bakrī, *al-Masālik wa'l-Mamālik*, 864–67. *Corpus of Early Arabic Sources*, ed. Levtzion and Hopkins, 74–77.

followers listened attentively to his sayings and recorded his teachings and opinions and that he exercised unique moral and spiritual authority, including the ability to chastise and punish the highest tribal and military commanders (which included Yahya b. 'Umar himself, and his brother, Abu Bakr). Until his death, Ibn Yasin wielded this supreme moral and political authority. He bestowed the movement's military leaders with their titles and articulated the political and religious theory that would grant the movement a legitimacy that would be acknowledged by the region's most prominent religious authorities, and by the greatest and most orthodox authorities of the Muslim World, in distant Iraq.

Military Success and the Almoravid Confederation

Ibn Yasin's considerable military successes over the following years handed the Almoravids control of the entire western Sahara and its most important caravan cities–Awdaghust and Sijilmasa–on the desert's southern and northern borders. This was not the first instance of Berber commercial contact and military activity across the southern edge of the Sahara (into the Sahel and the western Sudan), nor was it the beginning of religious or Islamic discourse and conversion associated with this activity. Islam had trickled across the Sahara through the development of a network of small communities of merchants and pious individuals, figures already present in places like Awdaghust. But the Almoravid unification of the western Sahara and expansion along its southern frontier was the fruition of such activity on a new level. The Almoravid expansion represented a more structured, political, powerful and hostile development, propelled by a sense of righteous struggle against the unbelievers of the south.[8] Awdaghust had been under the non-Muslim authority of the Soninke Empire. Yahya b. 'Umar and Ibn Yasin marched forty days south from Sijilmasa to Awdaghust and conquered it

---

8 Or at least this is the way it is narrated.

by assault, according to al-Bakri. This was sometime around 446/1054–5 and seems straight forward.[9] There is something evanescent about the Almoravid conquest of the deep south, however. The textual sources on the episode are summarized in the briefest report, raising the question about whether there ever really was a military conquest. Regardless of the nature of the Almoravid expansion south of the Sahara, it can be said with some certainty that the contacts and political relationship were of such a nature that they gained unparalleled access and control over economic resources that became the central pillar of their nascent state.[10]

Better recorded is the capture of Sijilmasa. This occurred over two clear stages, which took place before and after the Awdaghust campaign. The most important caravan city of the Far West on the northern edge of the Sahara, Sijilmasa acted as a gateway (or port) between the desert, the western Sudan, and the western Maghrib. This city was diverse for its size and relative provinciality, enjoying far-flung commercial contacts. It was ruled by Zanata Berbers, of which the Maghrawa tribe had ruled for 60 years. The Maghrawa Zanata were Muslim, but espoused a heterodox (or non-Sunni) form of Islam associated with Kharijism. Kharijism, in its Sufri and Ibadi groups, was the dominant form of Islam here and across the Sahara before the emergence of the Almoravids.[11]

---

9 Bennison, *Almoravid and Almohad Empires*, 30; Bosch Vilá, *Almorávides*, 60.

10 Islam took root and began to diffuse in the western Sahel as well. Control of the region around Azzugi appears to have been stable along with an eastern expansion into the zone between Sijilmasa and Waraqlan, through the Masufa, one of the Almoravid tribes related through marriage to Abu Bakr, Yahya b. 'Umar's successor as amir. The southern frontier zone with Ghana, where there is strong evidence of religious and cultural exchange, may have been characterized by partnership rather than conquest. Bennison, *Almoravid and Almohad Empires*, 38. Burkhalter, "Listening for Silences in Almoravid History."

11 The rise of the Almoravids displaced both these forms, bringing in the new Sunni orthodoxy they championed along with the tribal

These were important articulations of early Islam that were neither Sunni nor Shi'a, and share a concern for notions of membership and imamate theory (rightful leadership of the community of believers), crucially not espousing the Sunni/Shi'a ideals of descent from Muhammad or from his family, clan, or tribe as requirements for leadership.[12] In 446/1054, Ibn Yasin and Yahya b. 'Umar marched against the Maghrawa because Waggag b. Zalwi had beseeched them.[13] Demonstrating again his pervasive influence, Waggag spoke on behalf of kindred pious individuals living in Sijilmasa: Sunni Malikis who felt oppressed by a leadership they considered heretical (the Khariji Maghrawa amir, Mas'ud b. Wanudin). They seized a large herd of camels belonging to Ibn Wanudin before moving on the city. Once vanquished, Ibn Yasin purified Sijilmasa from heresy by removing objects and abolishing objectionable practices. He broke musical instruments, burnt down wine shops and taverns, and abolished non-Qur'anic taxes (common tropes of moral reform). He also appointed a Lamtuna chief as governor before returning to the desert.[14]

The Lamtuna-led confederation, bolstered by a powerful religious ideology embodied in a charismatic leader, consolidated control of western Saharan routes and replaced the leadership of the two entrepôts (or urban centres) at the poles of this network. This early Almoravid confederation did not take shape uncontested. The Guddala (first rivals of Ibn Yasin and the Lamtuna and whose home region was located along the Atlantic coast) rebelled at least two further times. Sijilmasa also had to be conquered once more, after the

---

groups with which they had been associated (the Zanata were displaced, at least in terms of leadership, by the Sanhaja).

12 See Adam Gaiser, "Ibāḍiyya," EI3.

13 According to one narrative tradition (including Ibn Khaldun, Ibn Abi Zar', and Nasiri: Bosch Vilá, *Almorávides*, 67.) Ibn Abi Zar''s description, including mention of the group letter inviting Almoravid intervention, can be found in *Corpus of Early Arabic Sources*, ed. Levtzion and Hopkins, 242.

14 Bosch Vilá, *Almorávides*, 70.

Maghrawa leadership mounted a come-back. And the southern border appears to have been afflicted with regular insurrections that absorbed significant energy and resources. These setbacks notwithstanding, Almoravid power was in the ascendant, and Ibn Yasin could push on from Sijilmasa, as the city grew into the movement's first capital and base from which to proceed north in a war of conquest construed as a contest against heresy and unbelief. The conquest of Sijilmasa (like the earlier contest with the Guddala) provided Ibn Yasin and his followers with an important experience and a precedent for how to grow in the future. The basic ingredients of Almoravid expansion and empire were in evidence: The struggle to overcome a power and ruler designated heretical and unjust at the invitation of a grass-roots initiative of pious men (with whom Ibn Yasin closely identified), powered by a growing hold over commercial routes, and the adoption of state-like gestures of sovereignty, such as the minting of the first Almoravid dinars. The conquest of Sijilmasa required articulating a basis of legitimacy for the movement. This in turn created forward momentum.

The two founding members of the Almoravid confederation would perish during these early years of expansion. Yahya b. 'Umar was the first to fall, at the hands of the Guddala, in battle at Tebferilla and before the second conquest of Sijilmasa. His brother Abu Bakr b. 'Umar replaced him as chief Lamtuna and military commander. After consolidating power in the Tafilalt valley (which leads from Sijilmasa into the High Atlas), Ibn Yasin, Abu Bakr, and Abu Bakr's cousin, Yusuf b. Tashfin, pushed to gain control of the other two valleys south of the High Atlas (the Dra' and the Sus). From there they moved into and over the High Atlas, home of the Masmuda, a major Berber group of the region, crossing eventually to the Atlantic coastal plain where they encountered the Barghawata. The character of the campaigning was mixed. Some communities were approached aggressively, as a war against heresy and unbelief (such as was the case in the Sus Valley and its main urban centre, Taroudant, where the little-known Shi'a community of the Bajaliyya were vanquished). But other conquests and alliances came about peacefully. This occurred as communities, often on the basis of tribal filiation, but sometimes out of convenience or in recognition of mutual interest, pledged fealty, as appears to have been the case with the Nul Lamta. The Masmuda communities in the High Atlas largely fell into this second category. They were won over relatively easily, finding common cause against another Maghrawa ruler who controlled a trade centre just north of the High Atlas, Aghmat, which the Almoravids took after the ruler, Laqqut, fled to the town of Tadla in 450/1058.[15] An Almoravid troop tracked him down two weeks later and slew him.

The second was ʿAbd Allah b. Yasin himself. From Aghmat, Ibn Yasin had endeavoured to push forward, against the Barghawata of the Atlantic plain, a group that epitomized the kind of paganism and heresy against which Almoravid reform defined itself. The Barghawata were nominally Muslim, but had a prophet and scripture of their own. And as with the Bajaliyya, it is difficult—if not impossible—to know what precisely these religious communities professed, since those who wrote about them were largely unsympathetic and tended to impute stock heretical beliefs. In a raid led by Ibn Yasin deep into Barghawata territory, at a spot known as Kurifala, some 30 km or twenty miles from Rabat (which would not be founded for another century or so), he was ambushed and killed, on 24 *Jumāda al-ʾŪlā* 451/July 8, 1059. Ibn Abi Zarʿ (d. after 726/1326), writing in the fourteenth century, three hundred years after the fact, describes Ibn Yasin being taken back to camp, where he spoke his final words to the Almoravid elders and leaders gathered there, exhorting them to keep courage, beware dissension, and persevere united in the defence of Truth.[16] Ibn Abi Zarʿ also writes that in his own time a mosque had been built over Ibn Yasin's grave, not far from where he was said to have fallen, the founder of the Almoravids thus woven into the spiritual landscape; his resting place remains a site of visitation to this day.

---

15 Bosch Vilá, *Almorávides*, 87.

16 *Corpus of Early Arabic Sources*, ed. Levtzion and Hopkins, 244.

Ibn Yasin had appointed as sole leader Abu Bakr b. 'Umar, who secured promises of allegiance in the following weeks. The nature of this leadership followed Yahya b. 'Umar's model, more than that set by Ibn Yasin, whose spiritual leadership was only briefly inherited by one Sulayman b. 'Addu, another student of Waggag who, it appears, assumed the mantle of imam (spiritual leader) for just a few months before also being slain by the Barghawata. Thereafter, no imam of the Almoravids is known to have existed, and authority became invested in the Lamtuna amir. Abu Bakr b. 'Umar was the first to possess this combined authority. Or, put differently, one might say that the individual spiritual charisma of Ibn Yasin became vested in the Maliki 'ulama' (the pious scholars) as a group, while Abu Bakr as military, political, and tribal leader, would assume functional leadership, as well as be invested with heightened religious authority, evident in his title, *Amīr al-Muslimīn* (Commander of the Muslims), which implied that his legitimacy rested on his patronage and respect for the religious-juridical establishment of Ibn Yasin, Waggag, and their successors. And while the figure of Ibn 'Addu was occluded by Abu Bakr and by the memory of Ibn Yasin himself in the historical writing of Morocco, he survives more distinctly in the historical memory in Mauritania and further south, where he is remembered, celebrated, and memorialized. This intriguing split in the historical memory of the region points to a deeper north-south division of the Almoravid world, in which the Lamtuna heartland and vital southern edge of the Sahara are eclipsed by the lands they conquered in the north (the northern Maghrib and al-Andalus) where the overwhelming majority of historiographical texts and evidence was produced.

* * *

The remarkable life of 'Abd Allah b. Yasin was the result and expression of a revolution, at root level, of the societies of western North Africa and the Sahara. Such a life would not have been lived without multiple elements coming into place nor would it have had the profound, long-term impact it had on the Maghrib. In these earliest stages of the formation of an Almoravid empire, Ibn Yasin's life-work shaped the core of the new state, which would bloom after his death on an entirely unprecedented scale, in a region which had been characterized by the absence of such structures and a tendency toward unruly independence and fragmentation. The relative scarcity of taxable agrarian population and land from which to accumulate surplus production had made the desert reaches obstreperous to ambitious leaders as well as to states and empires who wished to control them. Before the nineteenth century, the movement of desert populations was difficult to monitor or control. And before the Almoravid period, while there had been frequent commerce in and with the desert (during the Roman Empire, for example), trans-Saharan movement, commerce, and political integration of the kind evinced by Ibn Yasin's career was nearly unknown. Ibn Yasin's life and the foundation of the Almoravid movement thus represent a pivotal moment for the Maghrib and the Sahara, when commerce and movement between and across the desert grew dramatically, affecting the entire network of towns on northern and southern boundaries of the desert, bringing the region into greater contact with the cities of the north (such as Qayrawan) and the Mediterranean and its commercial network. This was a commercial revolution, at its basis, evidenced by the earliest kernel of the foundation story: in which a travelling party on the way back from Mecca—through Cairo—stops in Qayrawan on its way to the western Sahara. The story highlights the religious and scholarly dimensions of this exchange, but this kind of movement rested on the existence of regular commercial exchange and contact, with all the skill, knowledge, and shared practices that makes such regular exchange possible, and which occurred along a network that combined frequent short distance travel and exchange with longer-haul movement. This commercial revolution in the western Maghrib made the Almoravids possible.

Its foundations had been laid beforehand, beginning in the second/eighth century, during the earliest stages of contact and diffusion of Islam in the region, when Ibadi and Sufri merchants established commercial Saharan and trans-Saharan networks that traded with communities in towns such as Sijilmasa, Aghmat, and Tadart, which in turn traded with the growing cities of the Muslim West (*al-Gharb al-Islāmī*, a useful term), such as Qayrawan and Fes. The most prominent commodities traded along these networks were gold, salt, and slaves, but a variety of other goods and items were also exchanged, such as ostrich feathers and pearls. Saharan and trans-Saharan trade—with its roots in antiquity—did not develop overnight, but flourished gradually and in conjunction with trade in the Muslim West and the Mediterranean. By the middle of the third/ninth century, contacts are known to have existed between Ibadi commercial and political agents and the Umayyads of Córdoba (the most important state and dynastic tradition of al-Andalus, founded by a fugitive Umayyad from Syria who survived the 'Abbasid takeover in the east in 132/749). The Rustumids (144–296/761–909, an Ibadi dynasty centred in Tahart, in modern-day Algeria) sent gifts, which included slaves and gold, and envoys to the Umayyads in the 300s/800s; a Rustumid prince was even raised at the Umayyad court. Urban centres further west, like Aghmat and Sijilmasa, cultivated commercial contacts far and wide. Correspondence with Sijilmasa appears in the Cairo Geniza, one of the most important medieval archives of Jewish letters and life of the broader Mediterranean World. And Sijilmasa's origin myth credits a wandering Andalusi silversmith as its founder. The Islamic powers of the west were interested in Sijilmasa and had competed to control it. The Fatimids, an Isma'ili Shi'a empire that appeared in Ifriqiya/Tunisia and conquered Egypt in the fourth/tenth century, had attempted to conquer the desert city. And the Umayyads of Córdoba had exerted influence through a client tribe that assumed control of the city in 367/977.[17] So, while the towns and urban centres of the southern and western Maghrib could be fiercely independent and profess ideologies at odds with

---

17 Messier, *The Almoravids*, 33.

their neighbours north and east, commercial and political–diplomatic contacts had been established from an early date and grew over the years. One of the engines for this contact was the Saharan and trans-Saharan trade that these urban centres pioneered.

The origins of the Almoravids came about as the inhabitants of the western desert rebelled against the groups that had exercised control at the poles of the burgeoning network (Sijilmasa and Awdaghust) and thereby established control of the entire western trans-Saharan network. This movement then proceeded northward, from where much of the wealth was traded. As we have seen, it was galvanized by a charismatic spiritual leadership and a powerful religious movement that saw itself as a force against pagan and corrupted forms of Islam. The elites of Awdaghust, Aghmat, Sijilmasa, the Sus, and the coastal plain were targeted and removed by the military and missionary zeal of the Almoravids. The process of Islamization and conversion entailed is difficult to perceive clearly, as the textual evidence is largely Arabic and Islamic: a kind of unsympathetic ethnography combined with an equally hostile historiography, written from the perspective of a religious orthodoxy that didn't fully settle into the region until later. The historical narratives must be read critically, taking into account, for example, a tendency in Islamic historiography (and perhaps in any historiography which privileges a particular group or state) to focus on Muslim actors and Muslim issues and entirely ignore non-Islamic ones. Narratives of Muslim conquest are full of stories of Muslim protagonists against a largely silent backdrop of non-Muslims who, in retrospect we realize constitute a forgotten majority that has vanished into the background.[18]

---

18 This point is eloquently made in a parallel context by María Jesús Viguera, "Dhimmíes en crónicas de al-Andalus: intereses y estrategias reflejadas en *al-Muqtabis* II-1 de Ibn Ḥayyān," in *The Legal Status of Dhimmī-s in the Islamic West (second/eight-ninth/fifteenth centuires)*, ed. Maribel Fierro and John Tolan (Turnhout: Brepols, 2013), 199–214.

This was a religious and cultural landscape on the border-land of Islamization, where orthodoxy had yet to be defined, where there was rich diversity of belief and practice, and where Islam as a minority religion mingled with other beliefs and practices. The Almoravid movement—with what, in ret-rospect, appears as an embrace of Sunnism—constitutes an important chapter in the emergence of a new orthodoxy, as the religion and its institutions established themselves on a large scale, evolving into a majority religion in much of the region and as the religious and legal tradition of an imperial state. The most prominent sects or heterodoxies the Almora-vids battled included the Sufri Kharijis, the Bajaliyya Shiʻa, and the Barghawata. The first professed what had been one of the dominant early forms of Islam in the Maghrib, empha-sizing moral rectitude as criteria for membership and lead-ership of the community of believers (as opposed to Arabian or Hashimi ancestry; Banu Hashim was the name of Muham-mad's clan). The second, the Bajaliyya, are less known, but were presumably associated with one of the Shiʻa or Ismaʻili religious currents that had previously appeared in the region, in which moral leadership of the community was exercised by an individual claiming direct descent from the Prophet Muhammad.[19] And third were the Barghawata, whose prac-tices appeared beyond the pale, in possession of their own prophet and scripture, but still putatively Muslims. Together

---

[19] Most notably under the Fatimids, although the Idrisids presented an important variation. The early descendants of the Prophet, through his grandsons Hasan and Husayn (putative or real), did not occupy positions of power in their life-times. A series of movements and rebellions and smaller, independent states, from the second/eighth century, rose championing descendants of these family lines as an alternative to the emerging status quo in Damascus and Baghdad. The frontier regions of the Caliphate in the east and the west proved to be fertile ground for these movements. On the forms of Shiʻism (Zaydi, Ismaʻili, and Imami) and the evolution of Islamic sectarianism generally, see Christine D. Baker, *Medieval Islamic Sectarianism* (Leeds: Arc Humanities Press, 2019).

these religious groups represent a state of fragmented and decentralized Islamicate practice and an element of regional cultural identity in the form of a Berber-language scripture. (Later movements would champion other forms of ethnic and regional identity, including adopting forms of Berber/Amazigh as a language for preaching.)

The Almoravids contained the paradoxes and elements of these disparate forces: They were a force of Arabization in spite of being non-Arabic speakers (later claims of Arab origin notwithstanding). And their spiritual founder was characterized by a charismatic force that drew from local customs and connections, which can be perceived in his idiosyncrasies. He had more wives than Maliki law allows, applied his knowledge of the law unconventionally, and is credited with miracles or magical actions, illustrating some sort of connection with the divine. The culture of the religious outpost, the asceticism and armed struggle that Ibn Yasin and the Almoravids embraced would seem, likewise, to illustrate vividly the spirit of a missionary culture of the border—from which it draws much of its ethos—and evidenced in the movement's name: the *murābiṭ* or one devoted to *ribāṭ*, the action of settling the borderland in the name of the true religion and pursuing the path of God, a deeply Islamic practice here taking a decidedly regional form, in the far west of the Islamicate world.

Figure 2: The Road to Taroudant from the High Atlas, the view of the Sus Valley from the mountains. Photograph by Camilo Gómez-Rivas.

Chapter 2

The Queen and Her Kings

The queen of Marrakesh, Zaynab al-Nafzawiyya, stands out as an enigmatic figure in the early history of the Almoravid Maghrib. The basic details of her relations with the Almoravid amirs throws up many questions, prompting the need for rereading and greater clarification. Maghribi historical writers seem to have envisioned her as a symbolic figure for the conquest of the Far Maghrib and its riches—for what disappeared of the old order and what was gained—through the mysterious powers that she is described as wielding.

Zaynab al-Nafzawiyya

Zaynab al-Nafzawiyya was the wife of Laqqut b. Yusuf, the Maghrawa chief of Aghmat. Troubling news of the Almoravid advance had drummed steadily since the assault and capture of Sijilmasa. They had taken four years to conquer the Sus and cross the High Atlas, where the Lamtuna-led coalition secured allegiance from a group of Masmuda and moved over the mountains to the vast plain where Aghmat was the major market town. When the Almoravid assault began to look imminent, with the fate of Aghmat in the balance, Laqqut fled. When Ibn Yasin, Abu Bakr b. 'Umar, and Yusuf b. Tashfin first rode out onto the plain leading their troops, at the end of 449/1057, Laqqut had been determined to make a stand. But a first series of attacks followed by defections within his own ranks weakened his resolve.[1] He fled with a number of his men under the cover of night. He sought refuge in Tadla, a town ruled by the Ifrani chief of Salé, Muhammad b. Tamim. Zaynab, Laqqut's wife and queen, was left behind in her undefended city. The Sanhaja troops and their Masmuda allies marched unopposed into town. Zaynab lost little time and sent emissaries to Abu Bakr, suing for peace and security for her and her people. The surprising outcome of this overture, and the negotiations that followed, was the agreement from Abu Bakr to take Zaynab as his wife, which he eventually did after a series of campaigns that further consolidated his control in the region. She would become his co-regent. Zaynab al-Nafzawiyya was the queen of Aghmat; Abu Bakr had gained a powerful ally, with access and insight into the region and into a people foreign to the Lamtuna. She obtained continuity and stability for her town and country in return. And she would play a leading role in its future.

As with Ibn Yasin, Zaynab's life is shrouded in legend. Stories about her abounded from early on, echoing her influence and decisive role in a community entering a new phase of evolution. Zaynab's father, Ishaq, had been a respected merchant, who had come to Aghmat from Qayrawan, the city where Yahya b. Ibrahim and Jawhar b. Sakkum had inquired about bringing a teacher back to the Lamtuna. But instead of the Maliki network of relations that brought Ibn Yasin and Yahya together, Ishaq al-Nafzawi had moved among Ibadi traders, with strong tribal connections to the Nafzawa and the Maghrawa, prominent in the long distance trade network. Ishaq was one of the traders whose business had flourished as the caravan centres of Sijilmasa and Aghmat burgeoned (as noted in Chapter 1). Zaynab was brought up among well-to-do merchant families. She received an education, reportedly from an "old woman of the mountain." This would later enable her to play a role in government.[2] When she was of age, her family connections and personal magnetism

---

1 Bosch Vilá, *Almorávides*, 87.

2 Messier, *The Almoravids*, 39.

brought the attention of powerful suitors. She was concubine to a Maghrawa chief in Aghmat before marrying Laqqut.[3] Ibn 'Idhari (d. early eighth/fourteenth century), an early historical source, ascribed magical powers to Zaynab. She was "distinguished for beauty and wealth, had praiseworthy virtue and an original mind, and it is said—and God knows best—that jinn used to serve her." He reported that tribal leaders and elders had repeatedly sought Zaynab's hand in marriage. But she had always refused, claiming that no one but "the true ruler of the entire Maghrib" would marry her.[4] After conquering Aghmat, Abu Bakr b. 'Umar was told of Zaynab's beauty. He did not hesitate to ask for her hand in marriage. She agreed. Zaynab and Abu Bakr married in *Dhū al-Qaʿda* 460/September 1068.[5] And, the story goes, she then blindfolded Abu Bakr and took him through a succession of candle-lit rooms, full of gems and precious metals. She told him this treasure now belonged to him, that God had given it to him through her. No one would ever retrace her steps and find the treasure.

Marrakesh is Founded: Abu Bakr and Yusuf

Through Zaynab, Abu Bakr had obtained priceless influence in the region north of the High Atlas, a strategic position from which to conquer a region more vast than anything the Lamtuna had ever imagined. The auspicious marriage enabled Abu Bakr to overcome resistance from major tribal groups in the surrounding area (e.g., the Banu Ifran)[6] and to establish a regional peace that would lead to seeking out

---

3 The name of the Maghrawa chief was Yusuf b. 'Ali. See Bennison's note on different interpretations of his identity (one and the same as Laqqut; his father; or an unrelated amir): Bennison, *Almoravid and Almohad Empires*, 33n30.

4 *Corpus of Early Arabic Sources*, ed. Levtzion and Hopkins, 226.

5 Ibn 'Idhari's narrative compresses time, so that a process which took several years is reduced to a few simple actions: He heard of her beauty, asked for her hand in marriage, and married her.

6 Residing in the area of Qal'at Mahdi b. Tabala.

a bigger location to build a new capital. When Aghmat had become overcrowded, the shaykhs of the Wurika and Haylana (two important tribes of the town) complained to Abu Bakr who in response asked them to select a place for a new city. Abu Bakr had been "used to living with his brothers in tents" until he married Zaynab "and the inhabitants of Aghmat multiplied." A dispute broke out over where the city should be built, each tribe wanting it in their own territory and the right to name it (these two clans had wrestled for power in the past), until a group of elders—including some Masmuda—successfully negotiated an agreement and selected a neutral place: "a desert place with no living thing except gazelles and ostriches and nothing growing except lotus trees and colocynth."[7] Abu Bakr rode out with his army and the shaykhs took him to the plain of Marrakesh, the "desert with no living creature." They told him to build his city there, in the wild land appropriately located halfway between the Haylana and the Hazmira.[8]

This took place within two years of marrying Zaynab and would be remembered as one of his standout actions as amir. Abu Bakr rode out with the elders of the Masmuda on 29 *Rajab* 462/May 7, 1070 and began to build the new city. Its first building was a fortification known as *Qaṣr al-Ḥajr* (Castle of the Rock).[9] Everyone lent a hand, including Abu Bakr and his warriors. The fortress was finished in three months and

---

7 The quotation continues: "Then some wished that the city should be on the river Tansift, but he refused this, saying: 'We are people of the dessert, and have our flocks with us. It is not suitable for us to live on the river.' So they looked out this place for him so that the river Nafis should be its garden and [the country of the] Dukkala its arable land (*faddān*) and so that the reins of the mountains of the Daran should be in the hands of its emir during the whole of its life." *Corpus of Early Arabic Sources*, ed. Levtzion and Hopkins, 226–27.

8 There is some discrepancy about tribe names and ownership of these lands, with Wurika and Haylana as well as Hazmira and Haskura mentioned. Bennison, *Almoravid and Almohad Empires*, 34n32.

9 Or Castle Rock.

building continued, "each according to his ability." One Tur-
kin b. al-Hasan is said to have finished a house in sun-dried
brick (*ṭūb*), still visible in Ibn 'Idhari's day. In this way the city
gradually came together, a Lamtuna city, initially no more
than a camp, built "according to their own custom," far from
rivers and forests, in a desert place where they felt secure
and could defend their animals.[10] The bustling camp would
become the capital of the empire and would eclipse Aghmat and Sijilmasa; the first turning into a provincial neighbour of the capital; the second, more intriguingly, shrank
and was eventually abandoned a little over a century hence.
The new capital, Marrakesh, would assume the twin roles of
capital and foremost caravan city of the western Maghrib.
Located on a plain irrigated by the snows of the High Atlas,
which tower over the city in the distance. Lush gardens and
orchards were cultivated around the city to feed its people,
but its commercial lifeblood was the long-distance trade and
the spoils and tribute the Almoravids collected from conquests and vassals.

The foundation of Marrakesh would also be one of Abu
Bakr's last significant gestures as amir. The conflict with
the Guddala in the Saharan south had erupted, once again,
demanding his personal attention. As he and a group of work-
men were taking a rest from building a wall in the new city, Ibn
'Idhari writes, a messenger on a horse, his hair wild with wind
and dust, reported that the Guddala had raided his brothers,
killed many men, and seized much property and wealth. Abu
Bakr instantly resolved to travel south to seek retribution.
But before, he had to deputize someone formally to be in
power in Marrakesh and the north. The obvious choice was
his cousin, Yusuf b. Tashfin. Even more extraordinary was the
next step: Before departing with an expedition consisting of
two thirds of the Almoravids' forces,[11] Abu Bakr divorced Zaynab and deputized Yusuf. In the manner typical of medieval

---

10 *Corpus of Early Arabic Sources*, ed. Levtzion and Hopkins, 227.

11 Ibn 'Idhārī says the date was Rabi' II 463/January 1071.

Arabic chronicles, Ibn 'Idhari narrates the events peppered with direct speech and dialogue. Abu Bakr said to Zaynab:

> "I am leaving you on account of rebellions and wars. I cannot depart from you while you are under my protection, for if I die I shall be responsible for you. It would be best for me to divorce you." She replied: "Your judgment is sound." So he divorced her. It is said that he said to his cousin Yusuf b. Tashfin: "Marry her, for she is a woman who brings good fortune." It is also said that it was she who asked him to divorce her, and he granted her request.[12]

The gesture is extraordinary and a testament to Zaynab's extraordinary character and influence in her community. She did in fact marry Yusuf, after observing the *'idda* (a period of time after divorce and before which a lawful marriage may not be contracted under Islamic law) and very likely initiated the divorce with Abu Bakr. She chose to stay in Marrakesh and continue playing a major role in leadership and affairs of state. Or, rather, she began to play an expanded role, by mentoring and encouraging Yusuf—greatest of the Almoravid amirs—to broaden the scope of his ambitions. "She kept his hopes high, organized his affairs, and gave him abundant wealth, with which he mounted many men," writes Ibn 'Idhari. And Ibn Abi Zar', another eighth/fourteenth century chronicler, states more bluntly that it was Zaynab who ruled during Yusuf's early tenure: "She exercised his authority and directed his affairs and became the conqueror, through her policies, of most of the Maghrib."[13] With Zaynab's help, Yusuf extended his sphere of influence and his network of leadership. Her influence and guidance notwithstanding, Yusuf did assume the role with natural aptitude, busying himself with the construction of the city, especially the gates and walls of

---

12 *Corpus of Early Arabic Sources*, ed. Levtzion and Hopkins, 228.

13 "Until she died in 464/1071–2" he writes, with little explanation about the nature of her premature death, which contradicts Ibn 'Idhari's narrative: *Corpus of Early Arabic Sources*, ed. Levtzion and Hopkins, 247.

Qasr al-Hajar. He kept Abu Bakr appraised of developments, led successful campaigns in the Maghrib, and established a mint in Marrakesh that struck dirhams and dinars (silver and gold coinage) still in his cousin's name. He quelled unrest in Sijilmasa and brought in and attracted more alliances and supporters. He had a boy with Zaynab, whom they named al-Mu'izz bi'Llah.[14] He created a guard of mounted slave soldiers. His prestige and authority grew day to day. And, presumably as something regents were supposed to do, but also pointing to the fiscal needs involved in state building, he taxed the Jews living under his authority rather heavily, "gathering 100,000 *'ash'ari* dinars and over 13,000 [ordinary] dinars."[15]

News of his cousin's imminent return then reached Yusuf, who had by now become loath to the idea of relinquishing his position. Zaynab once again had a key role to play. She "read on his face" the uneasiness the news caused him. She told him she could see the anxiety his cousin's return was causing him, that she would support his decision to keep his position and devised a plan for him to do so: "When he draws near" she said, "and sends the men of his vanguard to you, do not go out to him...Give him quickly a handsome gift...He will not fight you for a worldly reason, for he is a man of good who will not justify the shedding of...[Muslims'] blood." To which Yusuf is reported to have replied that he would never go against anything she advised. When Yusuf went out to meet him, the manner in which he did so was easily understood by Abu Bakr: They met half way on the plain outside Marrakesh, and Yusuf greeted him without dismounting, contrary to custom and rank. He alighted. They sat on a burnous (a loose, hooded cloak, after which the spot became known) and Abu Bakr proceeded to relinquish his claim:

---

14 A regal title reminiscent of caliphal custom.

15 The meaning of *'ash'ari* here is uncertain, but, citing Maya Shatzmiller, Levtzion and Hopkins think it may refer to dinars worth ten dirhams.

"O Yusuf, you are my cousin and stand in the place of my brother. I have no choice but to help our brothers in the Desert and can see none besides you who can take charge of the Maghrib nor one more fitted than you are. So I depose myself in your favor and put you to rule over it. So continue to exercise your rule, for you are deserving of it and fit for it. I have come to you only to put your mind at rest about your country and to hand over to you...the dwelling place of our brothers and their homeland."[16]

Yusuf thanked him and offered his prayers. He assured Abu Bakr that he would continue to be consulted in major decisions. A group of elders and notaries gathered to certify the arrangement. Afterwards, Abu Bakr went to his encampment in Aghmat and Yusuf to Marrakesh. The promising arrangement was credited to Zaynab's good judgment. She had lent him the support needed for such a major step. The most successful leader of the empire's history thus assumed command, prompted and assisted by the queen of Aghmat. The partnership between Zaynab and Yusuf—like that of Ibn Yasin and Yahya before them—shaped the early state. Medieval and modern historiography has tended to celebrate Yusuf. But the intriguing details of Zaynab's life and influence stand out like the tip of something more substantial.

Abu Bakr Battles Soninke Ghana, Yusuf Builds an Empire from Marrakesh

Yusuf would rule a unified western Maghrib unimpeded (as Zaynab's legend had promised). He would not know defeat or "have his banner turned back by any king." The cousins' parting, softened by Yusuf's "substantial gift of richly caparisoned horses, weapons, textiles, slaves and foodstuff,"[17] and the gesture of continued formal symbolic submission to Abu Bakr's authority allowed for the latter to retreat honourably

---

16 *Corpus of Early Arabic Sources*, ed. Levtzion and Hopkins, 230.

17 Details in *Corpus of Early Arabic Sources*, ed. Levtzion and Hopkins, 231.

to the south to manage serious (perhaps even intractable) issues there. Never to return, Abu Bakr went to the Almoravid heartland at Azzugi accompanied by a group of jurists (among whom was one Abu Bakr Muhammad al-Muradi from Qayrawan).[18] From there he campaigned against the Soninke Kingdom of Ghana to the south (he was likely successful, although the nature of that success is debated). Abu Bakr died battling the infidels of "the Sudan"[19] struck by an arrow (according to Ibn 'Idhari) with his fate written on it (Ibn Abi Zar' says it was poisoned). This happened in 480/1087.[20] As with Sulayman b. 'Addu (Ibn Yasin's successor as imam), records of Abu Bakr's southern command at Azzugi are few compared to Yusuf's in Marrakesh (possibly because cities developed historiographical traditions, unlike towns and villages). And this, in spite of the fact that Saharan and trans-Saharan trade remained of central importance to the fiscal and economic well-being of the early state, presenting itself as something of a mystery.

In the north, Yusuf built an empire. He started with the structures associated with the Islamic tradition of state building. He instituted administrative offices (*dawāwīn*) and a new and more formalized organization for the army that resembled those of larger Islamic polities elsewhere. This was bolstered and diversified by the addition of slave and mercenary elements: two hundred troops from Sudanic Africa and two hundred and forty Christian horsemen from Iberia. His success attracted more Sanhaja warriors into the ranks, supplying the human and military resources necessary to launch campaigns of expansion and conquest northward. Yusuf and others of the Almoravid elite (which was concentrated in his clan)[21] gradually extended control over the region north of

---

18 Bennison, *Almoravid and Almohad Empires*, 37.

19 In earlier usage, Sudan denotes the entire Sahel, south of the Sahara, east and west.

20 *Corpus of Early Arabic Sources*, ed. Levtzion and Hopkins, 248. There is a date discrepancy between Ibn Abi Zar' and Ibn 'Idhari.

21 The Banu Targut.

Marrakesh, along the Atlantic coast and over the Middle Atlas, fertile lands with denser populations, principal of which were the Masmuda, the Berber Barghawata of the Tamesna region, and the Zanata Berber communities (the principalities of the Maghrawa and Banu Ifran), spread across the northern half of Morocco and east into Algeria.[22] From around 465/1073, Yusuf's paternal cousin, Mazdali, charged against Salé, on the Atlantic (across the Bou Regreg from where Rabat was later built), and Yati b. Isma'il pushed toward Meknès, ruled by the Zanata amir, Khayr b. Khazar.[23] Here—as was to become established pattern—messengers were sent from the Almoravid encampment to the town to negotiate terms of surrender. They were successful in this case, after Khayr agreed to submit with the other Zanata chiefs on the condition that they be given safe passage to Marrakesh to negotiate their terms directly with Yusuf. Yati appointed an Almoravid governor in Salé and returned to Marrakesh with the Zanata chiefs. Khayr was allowed to return to live outside Meknès. This pattern was replayed over the following decade with a series of variations as the Almoravids conquered and negotiated terms and alliances across the north.

Over the next ten years, Yusuf directed the conquest of the north largely from his base at Marrakesh, from where he continued to build and develop the administrative structures of government and as territories and communities were brought into the realm of the burgeoning state. Representatives of these communities, conquered or peacefully incorporated, would sometimes make the journey to Marrakesh to negotiate, beseech, and face their conquerors and new leaders in person. And the journeys and these individuals travelling—willingly or unwillingly—to the court of Yusuf, traced a new pattern of power and a new centre of gravity in the western Maghrib, bringing political and community traditions into a new orbit, restyling and adapting these to a new reality.

---

22 Bennison, *Almoravid and Almohad Empires*, 38; Bosch Vilá, *Almorávides*, 108.

23 Bennison, *Almoravid and Almohad Empires*, 39.

The conquest progressed through a combination of stick and carrot. Many communities capitulated early to avoid bloodshed, but some resisted tenaciously and were met with overwhelming force and violence. Within a year of conquering Meknès, one of Yusuf's cousins, Yahya b. Wasinu, marched on Fes where the Maghrawa brothers, Futuh and Dunas b. Hamama put up such resistance. The conquest occurred over two stages (as it had in Sijilmasa, according to Ibn Abi Zara').[24] After an initial and relatively easy conquest, in which the leadership of the city was compelled to flee, a member of the Zanata leadership (Tamim, son of Futuh's cousin Mu'ansar) retook the city, eliminating the Almoravid garrison. This was followed by a second siege and invasion, after a seven day assault, "during which they killed the Maghrawa and their fellow Zanata of the Banu Ifran tribe 'in the mosques and streets of the city'." When the dust had settled, Futuh and Dunas were given safe conduct to leave (*amān*) and the Almoravids had definitively taken possession of Fes—the oldest Muslim city and most important urban centre of the western Maghrib—a major addition to the realm, in terms of population, human and social resources, culture, and markets. The eastern Algerian town of Tlemcen and the Muluwiyya Valley (which with Fes has a natural connection via the Taza pass) were then conquered by Mazdali and his son Yahya in 468/1075–6. Tlemcen's Zanata ruler, al-'Abbas b. Yahya, travelled to Marrakesh to negotiate his future. He was allowed to return and rule under the authority of the Almoravid military governor, Yahya b. al-Mazdali. This kind of arrangement was also common under Almoravid rule.

The final expansion into the northern Maghrib unfolded over the next eight years or so, moving eastward and westward along trade routes to the Mediterranean. From Tlemcen, the road led to Ténès, Oran, and Algiers, added by the early 470s/1080s. And from Fes and Meknès, through the Muluwiyya Valley, and over the Riff Mountains, the road finally

---

24 Bennison sees a suspicious trope here. Bennison, *Almoravid and Almohad Empires*, 39.

led to the Mediterranean ports of Ceuta and Tangier, where the kingdom led by Suqqut al-Barghawati and his son Diya' al-Dawla resisted until 477/1084 (technically not a kingdom but a Ta'ifa, one of the city states that formed after the fall of Ummayyad Córdoba).[25] With the incorporation of this last territory, the Almoravids broke completely the hold the Zanata and Barghawata historically had had in the western Maghrib. They also acquired what became their most important port city (Ceuta), where Yusuf's son (and next regent) would be born, and from where they would cross the sea.

* * *

Under Yusuf, the Almoravid movement completed its transformation from desert movement (a tribal confederation inspired by an Islamic reformist and charismatic movement establishing control over a trade network) to empire, with a new and more complex identity and corresponding notions of belonging and legitimacy, capable of incorporating a wider diversity of membership and communal traditions. The Almoravids under Yusuf introduced a new pattern of government and society into the western and central Maghrib. This transformation is evidenced on multiple levels. On the level of state-building, it was visible through the creation of a series of administrative structures newly developed in the territories and communities of the Almoravid realm, as well as in the physical structures built and commissioned by Yusuf in cities taking on an Almoravid character, from Marrakesh— the new capital—to Fes, one of the Far Maghrib's oldest and most important Muslim city-state traditions (now absorbed into the empire). Other towns and urban centres also contributed to the composition of the new state. And most of them were transformed by the Almoravid unification, often acquiring signature urban features. Urbanization and inclusion into the new state went hand in hand, a process further associ-

---

25 Suqqut, former governor of the Hammadids, died in the conquest of Tangier. Diya' continued from Ceuta.

ated with the appearance of new institutions and networks of learning, government, and trade.

Yusuf oversaw the building of the congregational mosque of Marrakesh, a monumental structure at the symbolic centre of the empire. In Fes, he ordered the building of the walls, unifying the two existing quarters of the city—and thus creating a new city—and the renovation of the congregational mosque. These were buildings and architectural features of symbolic and practical administrative significance. The city's congregational mosque was a central feature both for religio-political legitimacy and for the administration of justice, even at a routine level. Many kinds of oaths were taken (upon which the system of law depended)[26] and the Friday sermon was held here (a prominent and focal performative speech act for the articulation of religio-political legitimacy).[27] City walls and ramparts gave definition to urban structure and layout (in the case of Fes creating a new conurbation by uniting two existing towns) and underscored the protective and coercive presence of the new administration and military. Further east Yusuf's armies founded the settlement and citadel of Takrart,[28] which, combined with the existing fortified granary (agādīr), became Tlemcen. Ceuta was likewise transformed. A port city founded in the Roman period, Ceuta had had a long history of interaction with al-Andalus. It fell under Umayyad sovereignty in the times of al-Mansur's expansion into the western Maghrib. Later, its Hammadid rulers had claimed Umayyad descent in an attempt at restitution, after the Andalusi civil wars of the early fifth/eleventh century. Thereafter it formed part of a small kingdom or state with territories or communities on either side of the strait. The city can be thought of as one of the Ta'ifas of al-Andalus (the city-states that formed after the collapse of the Uma-

---

26 For instance, from witnesses, in defence of claims, and in formalizing transactions.

27 For a work on religious oration, including the Friday sermon, and the use of Berber language in the later Almohad period, see: Jones, *The Power of Oratory in the Medieval Muslim World*.

28 Or Tagrart.

yyads of Córdoba). Even here, at the outer sphere of Umayyad and Andalusi influence (an older state and urban tradition), the Almoravid conquest led to significant urban development, with the addition of administrative buildings and deeper integration into the network to the south. Yusuf ordered the building of a fortress for the city. And ensuing population growth would require doubling the size of the congregational mosque.[29]

The Almoravid unification of the western Maghrib coincided and, in important ways, propitiated a major development in the urbanization of the region. As can be gleaned from the list above, a series of monumental and administrative structures were erected—some still visible today—transforming the shape and character of towns and cities. This transformation implied a new form of integration into commercial and administrative networks, which meant, among other things, that the cities of the western Maghrib began to be ruled and administered by the Maliki legal tradition and culture and in a more homogeneous way. (In some cases, this was new to the city, while in others it was an expansion of an existing presence.) This was accomplished through the formation of a new literate and administrative class, with the educational institutions that formed it (the *madrasa*, a school for higher learning), a transformation most starkly visible in Marrakesh and in the broader southern half of the Far Maghrib, where the institutions of this new orthodoxy (Almoravid Malikism) had to be built from scratch. 'Abd Allah b. Yasin had been, of course, a regional founder and champion and exponent of the tradition, but with his passing and the dramatic growth of the state into a population many times greater in magnitude, it developed extensively. Yusuf and his administration were instrumental in this process. They turned to his Maliki neighbours in the north and eventually forged a critical alliance. Ceuta would be central in this alliance, in many ways the most important centre of Malikism in the Almoravid Maghrib, as its extensive contacts with Andalusi Malikism would soon illustrate. Fes too had a significant tradition of learning and

---

29 Ferhat, *Sabta*, 128.

its incorporation into the Almoravid state cannot be under-estimated. Yet in the development of the administrative and learning institutions of the new state, al-Andalus would come to bear a greater influence.

Beyond this institutional dimension, archaeological evidence points to a deeper shift in settlement patterns in the Far and Central Maghrib, in which smaller settlements were replaced by fewer, but larger and denser ones. One of the motors of this transformation, beginning in the fifth/eleventh century, is thought to have been long distance trade.[30] To this we should add the process of state-building itself, which developed commercial, legal, fiscal, and social structures that reinforced the development of larger and denser urban centres. It is not a coincidence therefore, that this archaeological pattern coincides with the appearance of the Almoravid movement, the pronounced growth in trans-Saharan commerce, and the political unification with Muslim Iberia (which we will discuss in Chapter 3). The long-distance commercial patterns and flows, almost certainly, predated the rise of the Almoravids themselves. But the movement capitalized on this economic and commercial development and accelerated and stimulated it further by creating administrative structures to direct and control long distance trade and implement fiscal and economic distribution within the state.

Almoravid religio-political legitimacy, in turn, had to be articulated in a way more sophisticated from that of the early desert days. The new alignments forged by the Lamtuna tribal confederation, the network of cities, and the process of conquest and incorporation together necessitated the elaboration and articulation of Almoravid politics and its main legitimizing concepts and symbols, especially as the movement turned from local tribal confederation to inter-regional empire. The Almoravid state and its representatives emerged onto a wider stage, coming into contact with older and more sophisticated (and self-assured) traditions. Almoravid religious and

---

30 Boone and Benco, "Islamic Settlement in North Africa and the Iberian Peninsula."

political discourse had to speak convincingly to new interlocutors, both Muslim and Christian (who they would meet very soon), in Iberia, the Mediterranean, and in the wider Umma. One of the most visible signs of this articulation was borne by Yusuf ,when he adopted the new title: *Amīr al-Muslimīn*, a simple neologism that was recognizably Sunni but unattested in the tradition. It is familiar because it is calqued on the venerated and ancient caliphal title, *Amīr al-Muʿminīn*, borne by caliphs since the time of ʿUmar b. al-Khattab. And it intimates the strategy of legitimation adopted by the Almoravids as they entered their imperial phase, although there is disagreement dating back to the medieval historiography over when the title was adopted. Qadi ʿIyad of Ceuta, who wrote the Maghrib's earliest biographical dictionary of the Maliki school (itself a foundational institutional development), claimed that ʿAbd Allah b. Yasin had been the first to confer the title on the first Almoravid amir, Yahya b. ʿUmar. This underscores the legitimating power of Malikism: the founder of the tradition in the Far Maghrib shaped the new title and office (ʿIyad emphasized how the imam wielded authority over the amir, even disciplining him physically). Ibn ʿIdhari, writing two centuries later,[31] tells a different story, in which Yusuf adopted the title after a string of major conquests (including Salé and Meknès), when it was deemed by leaders and advisors that he needed a more capacious title:

> And in this year [all] the shaykhs of the tribes united behind the Amir Abu Yaʿqub Yusuf ibn Tashfiin saying to him: "You are the Deputy of God in the Maghrib as your right is greater than that claimed by any amir except for the Amir al-Muʾminin (the Commander of the Believers)." He responded: "God forbid I be called by that name. Only the Caliphs are called that and I am a servant of the ʿAbbasid Caliph fulfilling his call in the lands of the west." So they said to him: "You must have a name to be distinguished by." And he said: "Let it be

---

31 He appears to have been in possession of other relatively early sources, no longer extant, such as writings by the historian al-Safadi.

Amir al-Muslimin [then]." For it is said that he chose it for himself, and he ordered the scribes to use this name when writing to him or about him.[32]

The great twentieth-century French historian, E. Lévi-Provençal, thought the title was only adopted after Yusuf had taken possession of al-Andalus, needing to justify this action, and based on the idea that the Far Maghrib's unification was easily justified and did not require such a leap. This view ignores the fact that the conquest of the cities of the Maghrib involved as great a transformation and reckoning with new power as did the invasion of al-Andalus. Not since the conflict of Fatimids and Umayyads had such large-scale powers appeared in the region, and neither of these had managed to unify the Far Maghrib the way the Almoravids did. Regardless of the historical truth (which we may never know), the three versions agree on the import and its basic motive: The Almoravids had emerged as regional players alongside other great powers of the Muslim commonwealth, but they lacked the traditional marks of relgio-political authority. They were neither descended from the Prophet's tribe or clan or family. They were not Arab. Like the Seljuks—the first great Turkic Muslim state builders in the east and close contemporaries—these interloping ethnic military regional elites saw themselves compelled to argue for their place and value, framing it in new terms. Both empires relied heavily (and bolstered) the religio-legal establishment. They robustly patronized the 'ulama' and built madrasas, called themselves amirs and sultans, and argued that they were guardians capable of defending the Umma from existential threats, from within and from without. Yusuf, as *Amīr al-Muslimīn*, professed to be subordinated to the 'Abbasid Caliphs of Baghdad, as part of this formulation. A Maliki scholar from al-Andalus would later procure a letter of endorsement for Yusuf from the 'Abbasid Caliph himself. But this subordination was all but symbolic, a solution to the problem of sovereignty in the Islamic West,

---

32 Ibn 'Idhārī. *al-Bayān al-Mughrib*, ed. Lévi-Provençal, 4:27–28.

with Umayyads extinguished and Fatimids chased out. The Almoravid solution—like similar elaborations—borrows heavily from past forms, including local and neighbouring traditions, recombining symbols of power to create something persuasive and new.

Figure 3: Almoravid dinars. Rabat, Morocco, Musée d'Histoire et des Civilisations, Rabat, Morocco. Photograph by Abbey Stockstill.

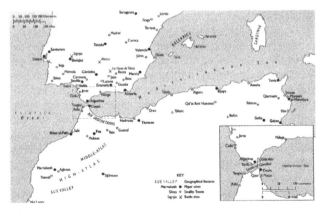

Figure 4: The Maghrib and al-Andalus, 1050–1250, adapted from Amira K. Bennison, *The Almoravid and Almohad Empires* (Edinburgh: Edinburgh University Press, 2016), xiv. Reproduced with permission of the Licensor through PLSclear.

Chapter 3

The Deposed

The last Zirid ruler of Granada, 'Abd Allah, wrote a unique first person narrative of the fall of his kingdom to Yusuf b. Tashfin. He paints a vivid picture of a complex process, contested by multiple parties and switching alliances. He portrays an Andalusi society that was deeply divided over the Almoravid conquest eliciting a wide range of responses from those who joined and championed as well as those who were deposed, co-opted, and absorbed by the new state, such as the author himself, last Zirid ruler of Granada, who would end up writing his first-person historical account from his exile in the heart of the Almoravid empire.

'Abd Allah's Loss of al-Andalus

When 'Abd Allah b. Buluggin al-Ziri (r. 456–483/1064–1090) inherited the throne of his kingdom[1] from his grandfather, he became the fourth and final successor in the line of Zirid rulers of Granada, in southern Iberia. Initially 'Abd Allah felt that a kind of stability had been established. But growing pressure from Alfonso VI of Castile to pay tribute and allegiance gradually undid him. Like many of his fellow Ta'ifa rulers, he tried in vain to balance looming threats as they closed in. He wrote:

---

1 Technically an amirate or principality, since the ruler was identified as an amir, but also referred to as one of the Ta'ifas or post Umayyad city-states.

The position was stabilised and each of us had full enjoy-
ment of his kingdom with nothing to worry about but the
external danger which threatened our countries from the
Christians. The peril was one to which all of us were equally
exposed. Although weakness prevented us from helping
one another, we used to exchange advice and views and
warn one another against something which might not have
been apparent to one or the other and so forth.[2]

'Abd Allah's position was that of a leader trying to hold on in
the face of two overwhelming powers. The threat posed by
Alfonso was felt first (compelling him to reach an accommo-
dation). But pressure and threats from Yusuf and his armies
were soon brought to bear, and from multiple directions, as it
was both a direct military threat and a source of internal dis-
sent, as Almoravid sympathizers emerged, voiced their position, and ultimately switched allegiance. This happened with
high officials close to 'Abd Allah's court and with neighbouring
rulers. The situation gradually wove itself into an untenable
crisis as 'Abd Allah tried to appease both giants. He paid off
Alfonso, while putting off official demonstrations of tributary
status and cooperation. He struggled with his own diplomats
whom he suspected of being duplicitous during negotiations.
And he busied himself fortifying his territories and defences,
physically, administratively, and interpersonally (sussing out
loyalties).[3]

---

2 'Abd Allāh Ibn Buluggīn, *The Tibyan*, trans. Tibi, 97.

3 He makes several preparations to withstand Almoravid attack.
But was at pain to reason that they were intended against the
Christian king and would be of good use for the Almoravids. "That
is why I put Almuñecar in a state of readiness. If the Christian won, I
would be by the sea next door to Muslims. I would hold out there as
far as I could until forced to cross the Straits and escape to safety
by the skin of my teeth and with a handful of goods and chattels.
It was with this object in mind that I had fortified Almuñecar as
was well known...God knows I had no intention of preventing the
Almoravids from waging the jihad. Although some think otherwise.

'Abd Allah's careful preparations were all for naught. When Yusuf and his allies turned their campaign against his territory, his defences, a string of strongholds and fortresses, fell away as his troops and commanders refused to fight and switched sides, pledging allegiance to Yusuf and his mission in al-Andalus. 'Abd Allah had no other recourse than to seek mercy. He abandoned plans of mounting a final defence, packed up, and rode out to meet Yusuf, accompanied by his mother, whose personal intercession through her family relations he hoped would buy him favour. Yusuf's ear (or strategic vision) leaned elsewhere; he showed 'Abd Allah mercy but stripped him of his possessions. Yusuf's local agents (Garur and Ibn Sa'dun) took inventory and searched 'Abd Allah and his tent. 'Abd Allah had to convince his mother to hand over treasure she had hidden ("she was terrified of becoming poor").[4] And she was coerced into performing the search and inventory. 'Abd Allah was sent packing with the meagre possessions he was allowed to retain ("three slaves, their mounts, and 300 dinars") from Algeciras in al-Andalus to Meknès in the Maghrib and into the custody of Sir b. Abi Bakr, Yusuf's nephew, where he learned that his brother (and rival) was also apprehended and sent to the 'Udwa (the other shore, as the Maghrib is often referred to). 'Abd Allah was eventually sent further south to Aghmat where he lived under house arrest, contemplating the course of events that brought him there. He wrote at length:[5]

> I now find myself less desirous of great wealth,
> once having had it and lost it, than before I
> acquired it despite the fact that my position
> then surpassed my present condition. It is
> the same as regards to all that I previously

I took a studied position of avoiding aiding the Amīr, and reasoning behind it." 'Abd Allāh Ibn Buluggīn, *The Tibyan*, trans. Tibi, 128.

4 'Abd Allāh Ibn Buluggīn, *The Tibyan*, trans. Tibi, 157.

5 I quote at length as the passage provides a rare example of a first person account and is rich with introspection.

attained, whether it be absolute authority or the acquisition of treasure or refinement in food, clothing, mounts or mansions and similar luxuries to which I was accustomed in my youth. So much so that there is nothing one could wish for or contemplate, which I did not have in full measure and even more. When I had these things, they were not suddenly taken away nor did they disappear within a short period of time and so cause protracted sorrow and be accounted part of my dreams. On the contrary, they lasted some twenty years and almost the same number of years before my reign since I grew up in their lap...Having lost all this, I find myself more eager for children than anything else of all I have described, for that was something I did not have before...It was a blessing bestowed on me by God that my first-born child was a daughter...God later blessed me with two sons, but I did not regard their birth as an occasion for rejoicing lest the worry for their future might coincide with my present misfortune...Then I devoted all my attention to the writing of this book—a book which assuredly does all that a son would do to preserve the good reputation of his father in the world—in order to make my position clear in the face of the confusion that reigns in the minds of the uninformed as a result of malicious reports which, the envious allege, led to my downfall. Nevertheless, I shall not lose the blessing which such reports entail, for, since I am completely innocent of the charges, I hope to reap the reward and blessings they can confer. I have in fact written this book for the benefit of people endowed with virtue and a sense of fairness which have been confused by the whole business, and who love me for no ulterior motives and wish me well...Furthermore, you [i.e., my detractor] have ignored all the good that I have done, every wise policy I have ever adopted and every service I ever rendered

the realm. You have looked for trivialities and
hunted out doings which entailed no disgrace
for the sovereign and no harm for the kingdom,
such as some moment of leisure snatched after
the performance of duty the sole purpose of
which was to reinvigorate myself, and other
such activities to which I had recourse for the
purpose of diversion...So all you can say now is
that the prince of Granada coveted money and
was fond of good-looking boys and their com-
pany as boon companions.[6]

'Abd Allah wrote concerned with defending his reputation
as sovereign and frustrated that petty accusations about
his behaviour would ruin his legacy, or worse, become all
that was remembered of him. This accounts for the efforts
at getting it all straight in his own account. But beyond his
individual reputation and ego, there is a wider resonance, in
that 'Abd Allah was writing about the culture and his frustra-
tion at its transformation, that the values he and his family
stood for had been swallowed up by a new culture and been
besmirched by the accusations of opportunists. The moral-
istic tone of these accusations, moreover, are significant, as
evinced by their echoes in other historiography of the period
and its tendency to paint fallen local sovereigns and leaders
of the frontier regions as turncoats, dissolute philanderers,
and drunks. This historiographical trope does indeed seem
to point to a change in political culture of the era. It shouldn't
be read too literally and would seem to point to a change
in political discourse and in the popular appeal of a morally
righteous leadership over an elite, cast as morally bankrupt.
Non-Qur'anic taxes, wine drinking, "good looking boon companions," and collaborating with Christian kings appear to
have been particularly powerful symbolic tropes in this rhet-
oric. The Almoravids were popular in al-Andalus and this kind
of moralizing discourse was particularly compelling.

---

6 'Abd Allāh Ibn Buluggīn, *The Tibyan*, trans. Tibi, 188–91.

Granada, Córdoba, and Seville

Granada had become an independent power in the aftermath of the civil war that destroyed the Umayyad Caliphate of Córdoba in the first quarter or the fifth/eleventh century (the war had broken out in 399/1009, and the office of the caliphate was declared defunct in 422/1031). The collapse had a shattering effect, creating a group of independent polities, several of which can be described as city states. They emerged from the fragmentation ensuing the loss of the centralizing power of Córdoba and gradually coalesced into about a dozen small states. These statelets are referred to, in Arabic, as Taïfas (sing. *ṭāʾifa*, pl. *ṭawāʾif*) and their rulers as *mulūk* (sing. *mālik*) or kings; as a group they became known as the *mulūk al-ṭawāʾif* or "party kings." Both terms carry strong pejorative connotations: "party" as in partisan, sectarian, and fragmented; "king" as in illegitimate, non-Islamic, and corrupt. The rulers of these polities would not have concurred with this nomenclature or title, formed retrospectively (becoming prevalent in the historical narratives that took shape after the period). They thought of themselves as legitimate, Muslim rulers, who aspired to replace the defunct Umayyad Caliphate, which in its heyday in the fourth/tenth century, had been one of the singular states of Europe and the Mediterranean (in Christian Europe perhaps only Byzantium came close in terms of institutional complexity, fiscal resources, and cultural output, textual and material). A tradition of emulating and aspiring to replace the Umayyads of al-Andalus is long in evidence in the wider region, with many if not most successor states in al-Andalus and the Maghrib adopting or co-opting some of its many symbols and institutions. By the late fifth/eleventh century, a number of Latin Christian and Mediterranean commercial and political powers (such as Genoa, Pisa, Castille and Aragon) began prodding their Muslim neighbours and vying for influence. This new landscape exerted powerful influence in the Maghrib and in al-Andalus (the Arabic speaking, Muslim-ruled segment of the peninsula) where these city-states vied with each other to replace the Umayyads and, like everyone else, competed for resources and influence.

Figure 5: The Palatine City of Madinat al-Zahra, outside Códoba, destroyed during the civil war and the collapse of the Umayyad Caliphate of Códroba. Photograph by Camilo Gómez-Rivas.

Sevilla had emerged as the most powerful Ta'ifa. The Banu 'Abbad, a notable family of Maliki judges, had become rulers there, assuming regnal titles of the Islamic tradition (such as al-Mu'tamid), and conquered and annexed neighbouring territories. The Zirids were notable neighbours of the Banu 'Abbad and had likewise emerged as one of the most viable Ta'ifas; they had emerged as a powerful cohesive military unit in the final years of the Umayyad Caliphate, having been brought into the peninsula as a fighting force by 'Abd al-Malik al-Muzaffar, the son of al-Mansur Ibn Abi 'Amir, infamous usurper-caliph of al-Andalus. They had come from Ifriqiya/Tunisia as a cohesive social unit, and they maintained clan and tribal identity (even keeping in touch with relatives in Ifriqiya). They were also Sanhaja–like the Almoravids–but of a different branch, associated with Ifriqiya, and so may have had little to no linguistic and cultural affinity, or at least we cannot presume that they did. When the Zirids were forced out of Córdoba during the war (in which they played no insignificant role), 'Abd Allah's great grandfather, Habus, consolidated his power base in Granada, and from around 405/1015 set himself up as ruler there, gradually securing recognition from neighbouring towns and villages. Habus's brother Zawi–also a military chief–had returned to Qayrawan when circumstances looked propitious for him and his clan there. He is said to have told his brother that they (the Zirids) would always be seen "as foreigners here." Habus, however, had no intention of relinquishing his hard-won gains in and around Granada, where he founded one of the most success-ful dynasties of the Ta'ifa Period. The Zirid leadership would be distinct (if not entirely unique) for owning and cultivating Berber ethnic identity. They cultivated a warrior ethos and an elite Arabic literary culture and Andalusi courtly material cul-ture, while staying proudly Zirid Sanhaja Berber and making little attempt to fabricate an alternate Arab genealogy.

It was under the Zirids that Granada first emerged as a regional capital. This was partly the result of the competi-tive and poly-focal nature of al-Andalus under the Ta'ifas (the centripetal force of Córdoba gone, multiple and surprisingly sophisticated urban centres, such as Toledo and Zaragoza, emerged in its stead).[7] Granada possessed a special combi-nation of resources (topographical, agricultural, and demo-graphic) that allowed it to flourish in the post-Umayyad age, when it shone in a variety of ways. Under the aegis of 'Abd Allah's grandfather, for example, Granada was home to one of the greatest exponents of the Hebrew literary revival for which Sepharad (the Peninsula's name in Hebrew) is so famous. Ta'ifa-period al-Andalus witnessed the most signif-icant burgeoning of Hebrew, as a secular, literary language,

---

7 Granada would grow further under the Almoravids, when it became the administrative capital of al-Andalus. And, of course, it would become the last major city of al-Andalus, surviving long after the Christian conquest of the other notable Muslim cities, which fell in succession between the fifth/eleventh and seventh/thirteenth centuries. The Nasrid Amirate of Granada capitulated in 1492, six months before the Jewish expulsion and ten before Columbus' landing on Hispaniola.

since its classical period in Antiquity. And Granada was a centre of particular importance, where Samuel ibn Naghrela (Shmuel Ha Nagid) was a major figure for Jewish history in the Peninsula, celebrated as a great statesman (he served as a minister and military leader for Buluggin. He also wrote one of the most important collections of medieval Hebrew poetry and set a model for later generations.) Zirid Granada grew and attracted a variety of talent, increasingly evident in later decades as it became a beacon of Arabic and Hebrew literary culture.

But the city was also infamous for intrigue and for political infighting, which routinely beset the court. So while Granada nurtured Samuel ibn Naghrela, it cut down his son in one of the city's worst episodes of anti-Jewish violence before the Christian conquest, when Joseph ibn Naghrela, caught up in complicated political intrigue, was murdered along with two hundred members of the city's Jewish community. Granada and its hinterland could easily become a powder keg, in which intrigue and competition quietly built up pressure. 'Abd Allah's Granada, a generation after the pogrom that took Joseph, was just as intricate and dangerous, populated by actors representing competing groups with complex ties to surrounding communities, who vied for influence in court and through the city's channels of power.

The Almoravid Conquest of al-Andalus

'Abd Allah lost his kingdom to the Almoravids swiftly and irretrievably and was left to ponder his fate under house arrest. When he sat down to write his memoirs and the history of his family, the sense of loss lent the narrative particular poignancy. Having inherited the throne of a flourishing kingdom and then seen it all fall away, 'Abd Allah was left to ponder his life and the legacy of his family in tatters. Under the watchful vigilance of his Almoravid guards, he packed his narrative with detail, doling out scorn and imprecation against those who he felt had betrayed him. He settled scores and tried to give the "true account," and, perhaps most centrally, he argued, vociferously at times, for the value of his and his family's culture and their place in the shared memory of a place that was being redrawn dramatically by the conquerors from the Sahara. 'Abd Allah presents himself as a proud Zirid Sanhaja Berber, a warrior and man of letters, possessing the kind of knowledge and sophistication associated with the most notable courts of al-Andalus, and worthy of a place in whatever emerged in the aftermath of the Almoravid conquest. 'Abd Allah also wrote his book for Almoravid eyes, who were unconcerned with his loss but interested in co-opting his experience into a new political assemblage, into their own library and story and structure of political legitimacy, where the memoirs of the last Zirid king of Granada fit their aims and purposes. In this way 'Abd Allah's book became one of the many artifacts the Almoravids collected as they absorbed the traditions and institutions of al-Andalus, a process that characterized the second half of the empire's life.

'Abd Allah had seen his position as regent and that of his kingdom as enjoying relative stability at the beginning of his reign in the 470s/1080s. He places much of the blame on the ensuing downfall on his counterparts and rival Ta'ifa rulers. He doesn't mince words describing their shortcomings. He calls Ibn Dhi al-Nun, the leader of the Ta'ifa of Toledo, a hypocrite ("secretly an enemy but outwardly a friend") and Ibn 'Ammar of Murcia a tyrant and a drunk, a wine-imbiber who rode rough-shod over his own people.[8] Beyond the characters of untrustworthy rivals, however, 'Abd Allah describes a treacherous political landscape, structurally unstable, where conflict (between the Ta'ifas) was endemic and the balance of power delicately poised. Al-Mu'tamid b. 'Abbad of Seville had defeated and murdered Ibn 'Ammar of Murcia who was replaced by a new ruler, Ibn Rashiq. Ibn Dhi al-Nun of Toledo had attacked Córdoba, killing al-Mu'tamid's son. 'Abd Allah's own brother, Tamim b. Buluggin, ruled over neighbouring Malaga (an important city on the coast), but their relationship

---

8 'Abd Allāh Ibn Buluggīn, *The Tibyan*, trans. Tibi, 88.

was fraught and Tamim proved a constant threat and irritant (among others, such as Ibn Hud of Zaragoza, another important but more distant figure). The relationships, calculations, and negotiations the Muslim rulers of al-Andalus performed were kaleidoscopic. 'Abd Allah balanced multiple bilateral relations, the arrangement of which would shift overnight as new alliances and conspiracies formed. Matters were further complicated by the nature and exercise of local power, as the Ta'ifas were based on coalitions whose shapes shifted. The power and interests of these rulers and constituencies cut across and interlinked local communities. 'Abd Allah's conflicts were not only or even primarily with other Ta'ifa rulers, but with individual members of his court and administration, who secretly negotiated against him and his interests.[9] The arrangement of his court consisted of a cabinet, with each member representing constituencies of unstable allegiance and under the sway of both domestic and external influence.

Whatever delicate arrangement there may have been was irreversibly altered in 478/1085, when the Ta'ifa of Toledo—a city of long history and rich urban institutions—fell in a bloodless coup to a Christian ruler. The coup destabilized the balance of power between Christian and Muslim states as well as between Muslim Ta'ifas (the two systems always interlocking). Overnight, the kingdom of Castile–Leon doubled (even tripled) its population. It now counted, for the first time, a large multi-lingual multi-religious city within its domains, along with all of the resources such a city brought, in terms of agricultural, manufacturing, and artisanal production, and intellectual skill and knowhow, a coup in all senses of the word. Toledo represented an enormous gain for Castile–Leon and its king, Alfonso VI, as an economic and cultural centre, but also as a symbol: as the old Visigothic capital of Hispaniae and as a sophisticated centre of Muslim and Jewish learning and culture. A city like this represented not just territory or labour but a resource complex at the apex of which

---

9 As he later accused one of his viziers of doing.

was the community's culture, knowledge, and skill. Toledo made Alfonso VI into a royal power to be reckoned with; the city's quiet capitulation reverberated far and wide throughout the Muslim West, striking fear in the hearts of the greater community, and especially of Muslim sovereigns.

The fall of Toledo set off a complex chain of events that led to the Almoravid conquest of al-Andalus. An internecine conflict of succession had prompted Toledo's leader, al-Qadir, to invite Alfonso into the city in exchange for recognition and support. In return for handing over Toledo, al-Qadir would be installed by Alfonso as ruler of Valencia. Alfonso himself had once been given refuge by al-Qadir in Toledo, as he weathered a difficult period at home. (Such an intimate acquaintance between Muslim and Christian rulers and their families was by no means rare.) As Alfonso's power grew, he pursued a mixed approach with his neighbours (not entirely unlike that pursued by the Almoravids in the Maghrib) in which he prioritized tributary recognition and allegiance from Muslim Ta'ifas in exchange for protection, and interspersed diplomacy with threats and violent and destructive forays. The quantities handed over by Ta'ifa rulers to Alfonso (and some of his Christian counterparts who pursued a similar policy) became considerable. Worried by this dynamic and its punitive cost, Ta'ifa rulers, such al-Mu'tamid of Seville, sought solutions with growing desperation, amid the mounting pressure from Alfonso and from competitors who could, overnight, forge alliances and turn. The fabled career of Rodrigo Díaz Vivar, the Cid, both in literary and historiographical forms (*el Poema del Mío Cid* and *Historia Roderici*) illustrates the arabesque political landscape of late fifth/eleventh-century al-Andalus/Iberia: a Castilian Christian hero bearing an Arab title and Muslim allies, friends, and subjects. Rodrigo Díaz was an autonomous warlord of the border region between the Muslim Ta'ifas and the kingdoms of Castile–Leon and Aragon. He played both sides of the religious divide forging alliances by necessity and custom (a practice only later questioned as unlikely).[10]

---

10 Namely, that Muslim and Christians formed alliances as they

Figure 6: View of Albaycín, one of Granada's oldest neighbour-hoods, seen from the Generalife, the gardens of the Alhambra. Photograph by Camilo Gómez-Rivas.

It is useful, and historically more accurate, to avoid thinking of a universal conflict between Christians and Muslims (between Muslim Taïfas and Christian kingdoms) and view the longer process, rather, as the collapse of an imperial structure (that of the Umayyads of Córdoba) gradually consumed by new state structures with power centres elsewhere, expanding from both north (from Castile, Aragon, Galicia) *and* south (from the Maghrib). The resource cultures of the Muslim city-states were the prize. Even when belied by a discourse of religious "civilizational struggle," the picture that ignores religion is probably closer to reality, especially in terms of how the process affected power structures and the economies of the Taʿifa states for which the Christian Kingdoms and the Almoravids began to compete fiercely.

* * *

fought, perhaps mostly amongst themselves (i.e., among Christian princes and lords, and among Taïfa rulers).

The course traced by 'Abd Allah would turn into a pattern, a physical movement of individuals or groups, as well as a historiographical trope, a way of telling a common story. The original template was set by the fallen leader: defeated and sent into exile in the Maghrib to face justice, doled out by the new power, followed by settling down far from where he could stir up trouble or draw on former loyalties. Here, 'Abd Allah wrote his unique account. But he was not alone in his experience, nor was he even the most high profile among such exiles. This distinction probably belonged to al-Mu'tamid b. 'Abbad of Seville, whose experience—as another prominent fallen leader and exile to the Maghrib—is often made to stand in for the fate of al-Andalus and Andalusis, for their political elite and their culture.

Like 'Abd Allah, al-Mu'tamid exerted his utmost effort to navigate the precarious situation (also pressed by Alfonso and Yusuf), and although he was more proactive he met a nearly identical fate. He led the Andalusi coalition in resisting and confronting Alfonso. And he was instrumental in recruiting Yusuf to the Andalusi cause (in this context, he is credited with the famous line summing up the situation: "better camel herder than swine herd"). He provided Yusuf with naval support in the capture of Ceuta and granted him safe conduct to the port of Algeciras (an Andalusi port) where Yusuf and his armies could find an operational foothold before setting out on campaign. Al-Mu'tamid rode with Yusuf into the Almoravids' most famous battle in al-Andalus, (the Battle of Zallaqa) where the Almoravids, defeated a coalition led by Alfonso after a difficult battle, an early and important success because it justified the Almoravid military and political presence in al-Andalus. Some of the many recorded details about this battle, fictive or not, are redolent with meaning for the fates and futures of its many actors: Yusuf cautiously opted to regroup and failed to pursue Alfonso's routed army. The heavy losses incurred by the Muslim armies early in the battle were caused by cowardly betrayals, stemming from discord deep within the Andalusi leadership. As a result, instead of staying to provide continuing military support,

Yusuf returned to the Maghrib where his officials and diplomats endeavoured to articulate a legitimate justification for dislodging the Muslim political leadership of al-Andalus.

When Yusuf returned to al-Andalus, he did so having secured the blessing of the Andalusi Maliki establishment as well as that of the Maliki 'ulama' of the Maghrib. Their successful co-optation was of central importance to the success of the Almoravid state and its administration. 'Abd Allah was the first to capitulate. Maliki judges, including some in his own administration, determined that 'Abd Allah's negotiations to appease Alfonso constituted a form of treason. Other Ta'ifa rulers, such as al-Mu'tamid of Seville and al-Mutawakkil of Badajoz, soon saw the writing on the wall.[11] They travelled to Granada to congratulate Yusuf, sovereign to sovereign, but they were snubbed. The historiography credits al-Mu'tamid with the dramatic words of realization: "We have made a serious error in inviting this man to al-Andalus. He will have us drink from the cup that 'Abd Allah has just emptied." The Almoravid forces promptly turned their campaign against the remaining independent Muslim city states, and systematically reduced them to submission. Al-Mu'tamid, the most prominent Muslim Ta'ifa ruler, defended himself proudly and doggedly, even as his territories and forces succumbed. Yusuf had returned to the Maghrib leaving Sir in charge of the campaigns with the strategic instructions of leaving the Ta'ifa of Seville for last. Sir then defeated Ibn Hud at Zaragoza through subterfuge and conquered Badajoz before turning on Seville's tributaries and satellites. Córdoba, commanded by al-Mu'tamid's son, al-Ma'mun, was conquered after its own citizens (echoing what befell Granada) turned on the city's leadership and delivered the city to Sir. Even so, al-Ma'mun fought to the very end, was slain and decapitated and his head paraded on a pike. In desperation, al-Mu'tamid appealed to Alfonso, who agreed to send one of his most able commanders, Alvar Fañez, to come to Seville's defence. But the Almoravid armies led by Sir defeated the Christian army

---

11 Messier, *The Almoravids*, 103.

sent by Alfonso (not without difficulty), and Seville was left surrounded as further Almoravid reinforcements arrived, led by commanders Abu Hanna and Hudayr b. Wasnu. Al-Mu'tamid and his family prepared to mount their last defence. Another of al-Mu'tamid's sons, Malik, was slain, and the city's inhabitants began to grow restless and desperate. Stories would later be told and written about how al-Mu'tamid put on displays of doomed courage, stepping forward without armour and just his sword, felling a soldier with a single blow to the head. In the end, he was compelled to surrender and was allowed to live after the unconditional surrender of Seville along with Ronda and Mertola (also governed by his sons, Razi and Mu'tadd).[12] Al-Mu'tamid complied and, like 'Abd Allah, he was exiled to Aghmat to while away the days thinking of where things had gone wrong, what detail of strategy had failed his city and kingdom. Al-Mu'tamid's sons had hesitated to comply with their father's capitulation. One chose to escape at the last minute; the other was betrayed and executed by Garur, the Almoravid official who had dealt with 'Abd Allah and his mother.

Al-Mu'tamid poignantly expressed the sorrow of exile and loss and fallen grandeur in poems that were complied into the literary history of al-Andalus. Like 'Abd Allah's contribution, it was a part of Andalusi literature written in exile from the Maghrib. There would be other writers—Andalusi exiles—that would give this perspective further depth and detail in ensuing years. And while the writings themselves of 'Abd Allah and al-Mu'tamid were anthologized, it was also their own personal narratives that would prove important, as additions to the cultural, social, and political history of al-Andalus and the Maghrib (and perhaps of al-Andalus *in* the Maghrib especially). Two and a half centuries later, when al-Andalus's most famous man of letters, Lisan al-Din b. al-Khatib (d. 776/1374), was exiled from al-Andalus's last burning ember (the Nasrid Emirate of Granada) as a result of court intrigue, he would pay homage to these illustrious predecessors. He sought out

---

12 Messier, *The Almoravids*, 106.

al-Mu'tamid's grave and composed a poem on the spot, on exile
and shared histories. He also found 'Abd Allah's history and
read it and incorporated it into his own histories and writings.

The narrative arc traced by these relationships and
echoes underscores an important dimension of the influence
of Maghribi exile on the history of al-Andalus as a whole: Ibn
al-Khatib's life and writings formed the core of perhaps the
most influential work of historical writing on al-Andalus in the
Arabic tradition (the early modern *Nafḥ al-Ṭīb* [The Scent of
Fragrance]). Written by the descendant of an Andalusi exile to
the Maghrib, al-Maqqari's book powerfully incorporated the
themes of exile to the Maghrib, and the Maghribi perspective,
into the historiographical tradition of al-Andalus and into the
historical memory of the community that cherished it most.
This dynamic and legacy of exile illustrates one important
dimension of the Almoravid conquest of al-Andalus, but
there are many others. The significance for the Maghrib,
and the Maghrib's centrality in the story, can be easily lost
sight of (since this is often told as an Andalusi story and not
a Maghribi one). This occurs, for one, because of the character of the historical sources: al-Andalus provided the setting
for the Almoravids' epic campaigns against Christian forces,
against forces who understood themselves as Crusaders, or
hostile infidels from the Muslim perspective. It would be hard
to overstate the importance of the Muslim–Christian struggle for the epic and related narrative forms of the region
in the Romance and Arabic literary traditions. The struggle
against the belligerent infidel and the defence of al-Andalus
provided the Almoravids with their most prestigious form of
legitimation, at least within the language of Arabic and Islam
(at a local level in the Maghrib, different forms of legitimacy
had to be articulated). Al-Andalus, moreover, had owned the
established Arab-Islamic institutions and traditions, including
a richer and more detailed tradition of Arabic historical writing. The narrative of Almoravid expansion, as a result, is one
in which a core group of Almoravid personalities battles relatively anonymous or undifferentiated groups in the Maghrib
(with the odd prominent individual), while, once in al-Andalus,

the story revolves around a much more complicated roster of individual personalities, intrigues, and struggles between Ta'ifa rulers and their courts and the Almoravid leadership. The quality of the story is different because a substantial portion was written by Andalusi elites. And because al-Andalus understood itself to be in the privileged position of the frontier of the Umma in its struggle against Christian infidels and crusaders.

With the Almoravid conquest, this story and the individuals who populated it began to be told from the Maghrib. It introduced the Maghribi perspective into the region's literary and scholarly traditions and (not unrelatedly) it accelerated the building of certain institutions in the Maghrib itself, mostly associated with state administration, scholarship and writing, religion and law, and material culture (along with multiple associated practices). Because, aside from compelling elite individuals into exile in the Maghrib, the Almoravids also heavily recruited Andalusis to their cause and to work in the different facets of administration as they created a series of new offices in the Maghrib. This is visible in the personalities of Andalusi courtier administrators who began to appear, and in the development of the Maliki institutions, which went from practically non-existent to populated in a generation, and can then be seen practising law and urban administration in the Almoravid cities (such as Marrakesh, Tlemcen, Fes, Sijilmasa, and Ceuta). The Almoravid conquest of al-Andalus united al-Andalus and the Maghrib for the first time since the days of the Umayyad Caliphate of Damascus, three hundred years earlier (during a time when all of these Arabic-Islamic institutions and structures had not yet been formed). The resulting flow of people and material between the two regions had deep social, commercial, political, and material impact. Indeed the material culture of the Almoravid cities in the Maghrib perhaps illustrates this influence best, as Yusuf's successor undertook a major program of urban development there.

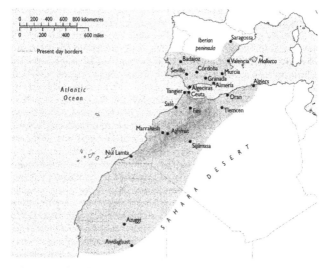

Figure 7: The Almoravid Empire, adapted from Amira K. Benni-son, *The Almoravid and Almohad Empires* (Edinburgh: Edinburgh University Press, 2016), 48. Reproduced with permission of the Licensor through PLSclear.

Chapter 4

The Son

The life of the second longest-serving Almoravid amir, 'Ali b. Yusuf b. Tashfin, provides a good vantage from which to contemplate the scope and scale of the transformation of the Maghrib under the Almoravids. While his father had inherited a tribal confederation with its heart still in the desert and a new capital in southern Morocco that was still just a military camp, 'Ali inherited something much more like an empire. Everything in his life before and after his succession underscores this fact, from his childhood in a Mediterranean port city, to the policies and major projects he sponsored, which have the highest profile, among Almoravid rulers, in the historical and archaeological archive, giving the shape to much of what was left to posterity.

'Ali b. Yusuf b. Tashfin

Yusuf was born and bred of the desert. Even after leaving, he had kept, one might say cultivated, the customs that marked him as a pious desert nomad (or pastoralist) throughout his life. He wore simple garb and drank camel milk into his old age. Or this is at least how he was represented, in a way which appears genuine to his origins, values, and the customs of his people. It was also very close to an Islamic ideal: simple, austere, and pious, a person of the desert in the way that Muhammad's aunt and uncle were remembered in the Islamic tradition. Yusuf's character echoes that of the Prophet as well as that of 'Umar al-Khattab, model ruler among the Rashidun (the first four caliphs). Yusuf's son and successor, on the other hand, was born of another world entire. 'Ali b. Yusuf b. Tashfin was born in a palace, in a city by the sea, to an Iberian captive and concubine of Yusuf. The status of such a slave/concubine changed upon bearing a child to a legal status termed *umm walad*. And as mother of a regent, she could bear significant influence.[1] The city where 'Ali grew up, Ceuta, was the Almoravids' most important Maghribi port, through which all traffic to and from al-Andalus (and elsewhere in the Mediterranean) passed. The city had always been an important port with strong connections to al-Andalus and the western Mediterranean. It had been home to claimants to the Umayyad Caliphate of Córdoba (who attempted a restoration in the early fifth/eleventh century) and had been connected administratively to cities in southern Iberia throughout the Ta'ifa period. Ceuta, in fact, can and should be thought of, in many ways, as one of the Ta'ifas themselves. Historically it is the Maghribi city with the deepest and oldest ties to the Peninsula. It is no coincidence that the Umayyads of Córdoba, at the height of their powers, had established their Maghribi foothold here. Under the Almoravids, Ceuta would develop considerably. It had its own homegrown scholars and hosted many as guests. 'Ali benefitted from their knowledge and skills, receiving the education fit for the successor of an empire and reared in one of its most cosmopolitan cities. This connection, to the city and its scholars, would show in his life and character as a leader. 'Ali b. Yusuf did more for the development of the cities and institutions of the empire than

---

1 Ibn Abi Zar', in *Rawd al-Qirtās*, identifies 'Ali's mother as Qamar (moon), who also had the title Umm al-Husn (Mother of Beauty). Confusingly, the anonymous al-Hulal al-Mawshiyya, identifies Fad al-Husn as 'Alī's mother and Qamar as his concubine and mother of his own son Sīr. See Ibn Abi Zar', *al-Anīs al-Mutrib bi-Rawd al-Qirtās fī Akhbār Mulūk al-Maghrib wa-Tarīkh Madīnat Fās* (Rabat: Dār al-Mansūr, 1972) and *al-Hulal al-Mawshiyya*, trans. Huici Miranda, 100 and 145; Bennison, *Almoravid and Almohad Empires*, 157; Bosch Vilá, *Almorávides*, 225

any other Almoravid leader. If Yusuf conquered the territories and populations that would constitute the empire, 'Ali built its cities, its high offices and administration, and its social and physical infrastructure. Most of what is left physically of the dynasty is directly attributable to him.

'Ali had not been the natural or obvious successor to Yusuf amongst his siblings. He had plenty of competition, which would trouble him in his first year as regent. But he survived this challenge and emerged as the first dynastic successor of the Banu Targut dynasty of the Almoravid empire. This constituted a distinct shift from the past, in which cousins had succeeded each other and after "secular" leadership replaced the charismatic founder. There had not been a tradition of father-to-son succession in the Almoravid state nor in its Lamtuna and Guddala precursor federations, in which matrilineal descent was commonly observed. It was a political innovation, most likely connected to the character of the new state, as it articulated its presence and legitimacy in regionally and Islamically recognized forms (espousing the patriarchal, father-to-son arrangements espoused by the classic Umayyad and 'Abbasid Caliphates). The choice of 'Ali as successor, which Yusuf announced in 496/1103, and carefully prepared for, bucked the tradition of leadership within a ruling elite that remained closely connected with a core group of Lamtuna clans. Yusuf died on 3 Muharram 500/September 4, 1106 in Marrakesh. Yusuf offered his mantle to 'Ali on his death bed, and his half brother, Tamim (Zaynab's son), placed it on his shoulder, and proclaimed him, holding up his hand: "Stand and salute the *Amīr al-Muslimīn*."[2] The first contestation of 'Ali's power would come, predictably, from an individual owning a claim according to Sanhaja kinship practices. When 'Ali sent emissaries to announce Yusuf's death and his own impending assumption of power, all of them returned with endorsements of loyalty except from his nephew, Yahya b. Abi Bakr, governor of Fes, who had been appointed by Yusuf himself. 'Ali saw himself compelled to march on Fes to

---

2 Messier, *The Almoravids*, 121.

subdue his nephew, having just taken the reins of power at the relatively young age of twenty-three. Yahya attempted to recruit and mobilize widely, but once 'Ali and his forces were camped outside the city, Yahya understood the weakness of his position and fled east to Tlemcen, where Mazdali b. Tilankan took him in and later negotiated his surrender and reconciliation, after a period of exile when Yahya was allowed, perhaps encouraged, to go on hajj (pilgrimage to Mecca) and would be pardoned upon returning.

With possession of Fes, 'Ali consolidated his succession and set about building the empire. This included (quite naturally for this kind of polity) regular military action to make his presence felt across the territories and communities of the empire. The reigns of successful and legitimate sovereigns are often portrayed (in the contemporary and later historiography, chronicles of battles and sieges and lists of those conquered and made vassals) as a succession of such campaigns, a kind of narrative representation of sovereignty and claims staked. These yearly campaigns would serve real logistical, military objectives, but, equally important, would perform as symbolic performances of authority, a physical and social way of making prerogatives, rights, and powers known and reminded. Performances of such scale and regularity were new in the western Maghrib and influential in terms of creating these patterns (which were state structures in and of themselves). And certain locations tended to be more obdurate and pose recurrent challenges. Some of the most prominent of these were located in border regions, such as Valencia and Zaragoza in al-Andalus and Bougie in the eastern Maghrib, and they could absorb a greater deal of energy and resources.

'Ali's Building Program of the Almoravid State

'Ali's most profound and visible impact on the Maghrib, as a ruler, was as a builder. As noted above, many of the extant physical remains of the Almoravid State were commissioned by 'Ali. Much of the direct textual evidence, moreover, was also commissioned by 'Ali or produced under his aegis (meaning that the texts survive, written by contemporaries of 'Ali, in which he is mentioned directly or indirectly, whereas most of the texts concerning Yusuf come from a narrative tradition that developed later and over generations). A few examples of these will follow, but it can be noted that one of the reasons for this difference, is that 'Ali built the social, administrative, and bureaucratic institutions of the Almoravid Maghrib and therefore a richer paper trail survives, bearing further witness to his influence as the second longest serving ruler of the Almoravid state. This is not to put too fine a point on a black-and-white distinction between the two rulers. Yusuf also built. And the continuity between them was equally significant to the development of the institutions of state. But the conditions were propitious under 'Ali for a wider scale of construction; the foundations had been set.

During 'Ali's time as Almoravid amir, the congregational mosque of Ceuta doubled in size. The great mosque of Tlemcen was built. The city walls of Fes were erected and the city's congregational and university mosque, the Qarawiyyin, was expanded. The port of Salé was built. And Sijilmasa, the caravan city on the desert edge, in the Tafilalt valley, reached its largest footprint. 'Ali's influence on urbanization is perhaps nowhere more visible than in Marrakesh. The city Abu Bakr had founded and the foundations of which Yusuf had laid, was given by 'Ali most of its oldest standing structures. He commissioned a palace and, most significantly, a new congregational mosque (it would be demolished by the ensuing dynasty). A smaller mosque, the oldest in the city, was also commissioned by him and bears his name. 'Ali had the walls of Marrakesh built, a process which included conceiving and designing the urban space as a coherent whole. Urban planning and development of the imperial capital involved significant infrastructure, one of the best known of which included a series of hydraulic works, used to distribute water for residential and horticultural use. Under 'Ali, the city completed the transition from military encampment to imperial capital, a process likely envisaged by Yusuf but only realized by his son. The city came to embody the wider regional impact of Almoravid state formation, through the urban development associated with the social and political structures of empire and Islamic religious and administrative institutions. State and imperial development and expansion are often conceived horizontally (as in expanding borders), but an equally significant vertical and local development took place, in a way in which larger portions of the population, including that of the countryside, came into more frequent contact with ruling and administrative offices developed in Marrakesh and Fes and the other administrative and economic centres, directly and indirectly created by the Almoravid state. Economic development included the development of manufacturing centres, such as the tannery neighbourhood, which brought hides from across the region for manufacture into a host of items. Artisanal production on this level required a degree of investment in city and municipal infrastructure and social organization, perhaps most crucial of which was the system of water distribution and waste management. Leather crafts manufacture entailed commercial space for exchange alongside other crafts (such as textiles and metallurgy) and a wide variety of foodstuffs and products for domestic use. The markets of Marrakesh, and the craft and manufacturing centres that produced the bulk of the goods exchanged, were a product of the Almoravid period. Markets and their fluid operation require a significant degree of supervision and state and community investment. The development of the city thus took place on multiple levels: from the mundane to the monumental. Naturally, 'Ali did not single-handedly direct or micromanage all of this, but concrete evidence of administrative interaction does show a significant degree of involvement on his part and a degree of personal investment.

Two surviving objects illustrate the material and symbolic impact of 'Ali's patronage. The first was made of wood and commissioned from master artisans in Córdoba: this was a stepped pulpit or *minbar*, which looks like a narrow staircase leading up to the wall on one side of the *miḥrab* (or prayer niche), which congregants face during prayer. This *minbar*

Figure 8: The Almoravid Minbar commissioned by ʻAli b. Yusuf for the Great Mosque of Marrakesh: wood and ivory, ca. 1125–1130, al-Badiʻ Palace, Marrakesh (Morocco). Photograph by Abbey Stockstill.

(later designated the Kutubiyya Minbar) was commissioned by the amir for the congregational mosque of the imperial capital—perhaps the most symbolically important and prestigious building of the state, combining political and religious symbolism with practical administrative (and scholarly) functions. The Kutubiyya Minbar is one of the finest surviving works of wood craftsmanship of such antiquity, consisting of thousands of pieces of wood and ivory inlay. Built by Córdoba's master craftsmen, it embodies the material and technical exchange between al-Andalus and the Maghrib that took place under the aegis of the Almoravids and under 'Ali most notably. As one of the focal objects in every congregational mosque—going back to the example of the Prophet's mosque in Medina—the *minbar* encapsulates the symbolic and functional importance of the Andalusi-Maghribi exchange for the legitimation of the empire. This cannot be overemphasized.

'Ali commissioned the Kutubiyya Minbar for the central monumental structure of the empire, a structure that invoked an Islamic tradition of spirituality, justice, and just rule, and expressed how the Almoravid movement and its leadership fit into this tradition, with its promise of justice and salvation. Unfortunately, and as noted above, 'Ali's congregational mosque did not survive the Almohad zeal for erasing the trace of their predecessors. When they took Marrakesh and made it their capital, the Almohads razed the structure. They demolished and built a new one in the same spot, precisely to manage and remake the symbolic power of the building. A small part of the original Almoravid building survives, however, which brings us to the second object, and modest as it is, it also bears witness to an important development. Qubbat al-Ba'diyyin is a simple but elegant domed structure that provided shade over the fountain in the ablutions courtyard of the Almoravid congregational mosque. It is striking for being the first of its kind in the region and the city's oldest standing structure. Its exterior is relatively simple: an arched base supports walls carrying a ribbed dome, the interior of which is beautifully decorated with patterns leading to lobed corners. Its antiquity in itself makes the structure a priceless remnant of the city's earliest history. But for a broader regional significance, the structure provides proof of the birth of a new decorative and architectural style: Andalusi-inflected, pan-Maghribi, and the first of its kind. Put in other words, the administrative unification of the Western Maghrib and al-Andalus and the commercial and material exchange entailed produced a new architectural and decorative vernacular. From this vernacular a direct line

Figure 9: Qubbat al-Baʿdiyyin, the fountain in the ablutions court of the great mosque commissioned by ʿAli b. Yusuf, from the outside. Photograph by Camilo Gómez-Rivas.

Figure 10: Qubbat al-Baʿdiyyin, the structure from the inside. Photograph by Camilo Gómez-Rivas.

to later Maghribi styles can be traced. This is significant for a variety of reasons, but a key one is to note that this structured material exchange with the Peninsula, the Mediterranean, and the wider Islamic World, had specific and striking material, visual, and cultural impact on the Maghrib (a material process so often obscured by abstractions and ideas, whether religious or secular, in the historiography).

The relationship with al-Andalus was of profound significance for Maghribi administrative elites and their literary and material vernaculars. The regional prestige of the Umayyad Caliphal style, expressed in the *minbar* and the *qubba*, bears witness to this. The literary evidence is equally striking (as 'Abd Allah and al-Mu'tamid's examples show). It is important to underscore, however, that the connection with al-Andalus was not the only regional relationship of significance for the Maghrib in this period. The relationship with Ifriqiya remained important. And the one on which the foundations of the movement rested, based on desert commerce (described in Chapter 1), continued to be fundamental throughout most of the empire's history. It is when considered together–the Andalusi and Mediterranean commercial and material exchanges combined with the trans-Saharan one—that the economic scale and power can be perceived. Indeed, the Almoravid period gave rise to the golden age of trans-Saharan commerce. Caravans of as many as two thousand camels regularly connected a web of towns and points of exchange throughout the desert and the Sahel. This type of commercial exchange coincided with the rise of the Berber Islamic empires before the disruption of European colonialism. It was a powerful material and cultural force in the Maghrib and in West Africa, where it led directly and indirectly to Islamization and the rise of bureaucratic elites and new states. The widespread fame and popularity of the Almoravid gold coin, the currency's name being adopted in a variety of neighbouring languages (e.g., *marvedí*), illustrates how the wealth produced by this exchange rippled far beyond the border of the Almoravid state.

The high point of this development, especially the one involving commercial exchange (as opposed to that generated by conquest), occurred under 'Ali's watch. This led, in turn, and in a way that was of crucial significance to the Maghrib, to the development of bureaucratic institutions in the Maghrib itself: administrative elites, local administrative practices, educational institutions and practices, and local and regional networks of judicial and administrative officials. An entire generation of literate scholars and administrators was planted under Yusuf and blossomed under 'Ali. The new literate class populated a variety of forms of literate production and exchange, including basic teaching, higher education, judicial councils, notarial functions, and other municipal offices. The appearance of this new generation of men and women of letters is attested to in the corpus of judicial writings from the region. In one famous compendium of judicial opinions (from the third/ninth to the early ninth/fifteenth century and which preserves the names of many of the respondents and consultants), they only appear in the Western Maghrib beginning in the Almoravid period, when a modest number of named jurists are first mentioned. There appear practically none before then. Scholars and jurists from al-Andalus and Ifriqiya, by contrast, are mentioned in the hundreds. Requesting and formulating legal opinions was one of the principal ways in which Islamic law developed and adapted over time. And it is not that there were no literate individuals and jurists in the Western Maghrib before the Almoravids. Centres of learning existed. But the scale of the Almoravid enterprise was different and brought Far Maghribi scholars and literate circles more into line with its neighbours, in terms of religious and legal practice. This rise coincides with the region's transformation from a collection of heterodox communities to a more homogenous orthodoxy.

The Sunni Revival

These developments under 'Ali were part of a wider pan-Maghribi transformation, often identified as the Sunni Revival which could more aptly be termed the neo-Sunni Revival, because it involved the formulation of new and original practices, organizations, and ideas. In the east, this transformation was identified with the Seljuks (the first large-scale Muslim Turkic state in Anatolia, Syria, and Iraq) and the Ayyubids in Egypt (founded by a Kurdish military leader who had fought for the Seljuks in the Levant: Salah al-Din, the famous Saladin). In the west, this work was carried out by the Almoravids. These three dynasties share in common that they represented the appearance of new non-Arab and non-Persian political and military elites, a kind of "Barbarian invasion" linked to the formulation of new political and communal identities and, perhaps more difficult to generalize, the restructuring of economic and fiscal systems of state. Formulating strategies of legitimation for these new elites was at the core of this process, styling Yusuf b. Tashfin, Nizam al-Din Mulk, and Salah al-Din al-Ayyubi, as legitimate representatives, champions, and defenders of the Umma. None possessed the characteristics and credentials that were central to older claims of political legitimacy of Muslim leaders, most notably a lack of kin relationship to the founding Arab tribes and founding clans of Islam. A new kind of leadership, a new religio-political community, and an attendant new kind of social contract slowly took shape. The new formation is most often associated with the term sultan, and we can call it a "sultanic" form of government for convenience: but it was a political and social transformation that went well beyond the identity of central leadership and informed the structure, and even the physical shape, of Islamic communities and their towns and cities, such as Damascus, Cairo, Fes, and Marrakesh.[3] Indeed, much of the visible urban core of these cities was built during and after this Sunni Revival and bears the marks of its culture and maps the social relationships implicit in the new religio-political formation.

Some of these forms can mistakenly be associated with "classical" Islamic civilization, pointing to their profound influ-

---

3 This point is put in a similar way in Amira K. Bennison, "Relations between Rulers and Ruled in the Medieval Maghrib: The 'Social Contract' in the Almoravid and Almohad Centuries, 1050-1250," *Comparative Islamic Studies* 10, no. 2 (2014): 137–56.

ence and centrality, but also to the complex layering of cultural development. These include the widespread popularity of the madrasa as a centre of higher learning. Baghdad's Nizamiyya is a good example: patronized by a Seljuk sultan, the Nizamiyya madrasa employed perhaps the single most influential Muslim thinker of this Sunni Revival: Abu Hamid al-Ghazali, who gave expression to several of the period's concerns, including the popularization and mainstreaming of mystical forms associated with Sufism and, more broadly, with themes of piety and popular spirituality. The new centrality of the madrasa was also associated with the greater definition (doctrinal, procedural, and institutional) of the Sunni Schools of Law. In fact, the entire idea that Sunni Islam consists of four schools (or *madhhabs*) was a formulation of this period, characterized by the emergence of a new Sunni orthodoxy after the flowering of a variety of Shi'i and Isma'ili dynasties in the century or two prior. The Ayyubids snuffed out the Fatmids. The Seljuks zealously persecuted and quashed Isma'ili ideas and communities (al-Ghazali gave stark expression to these doctrinal anti-Shi'i ideas). The Almoravids brought this phenomenon to the western Maghrib, where they warred against the local forms of religious expression, later described as heterodox: the Barghawata, the Bajaliyya, and the Midrarids.

In this context, it is easier to see how the Sunni Schools of Law are much more than juridical identities and procedural patterns: they are closely identified with religious identity, doctrine, and belief. They are also strongly connected to the establishment or principal tradition of higher education and literacy, and, therefore, they are intertwined with state administration and scholarship more broadly (i.e., with the cultivation of written culture). Some of the urban structures that housed these institutions still stand today, perhaps most famously in the Ayyubid and Mamluk cities of Aleppo, Damascus, Alexandria, and Cairo, where one can visit the imposing complexes housing madrasas, dormitories, study halls, mosques, and *khanqas* (Sufi complexes) and hospitals and a host of other charitable institutions. The complexes included shrines and mausolea to members of patron families and were often connected to agrarian and commercial property, the profit of which was committed, by means of a legal instrument (creating an inalienable endowment), to the upkeep of the institution's main function: room and board for students, books for mosques and madrasas, food for charities, etc. The Almoravid transformation of the Maghrib shared many characteristics with this wider movement of articulating a new religious orthodoxy and political contract and the associated emergence of new popular religious movements that channelled powerful and novel spiritual creativity within the framework provided by the new orthodoxy, although not always as successfully.

The Far Maghrib was a very different place from Egypt and Syria. It lacked the dense layers of urban community and associated traditions of government and state structures. It lacked a central and large agricultural area (fed by a major river, such as the Nile Delta), on which to build a typical agrarian state, capturing agricultural surplus and taxing the peasantry. This makes the urban transformation initiated by the Almoravid period all the more salient, a process continued by the succeeding dynasty, so that several major urban centres (later identified as the imperial cities) were founded or greatly developed in the Almoravid century and in the one following (Marrakesh, Rabat, and Meknès, founded and/or greatly expanded). The physical infrastructure, as noted above, is intimately connected to a series of social organizations, which emerged in our period and under the direct support and patronage of the Almoravid leadership. Again, 'Ali stood out in this respect, appearing in direct correspondence with the leading representatives of this new establishment. One pertinent example is 'Ali's correspondence with one of the architects of the Sunni Revival in the west, particularly in its legal dimension, through the theoretical elaboration of Malikism: Ibn Rushd al-Jadd (grandfather of the famous philosopher Averroës).

In a collection of specialized legal correspondence from the time (a *fatwā* or responsa collection) we find two questions posed by 'Ali (or by his secretaries) to Ibn Rushd al-Jadd. These touched on matters of deep significance to Almoravid state policy and of unquestionable symbolic importance. Ibn Rushd was a Córdoban jurist, where his family had deep roots and where he served in the highest judicial capacity (chief judge of the city) and was also widely known for his scholarship, including commentaries on the most important texts and compendia of the Maliki School. One such work was on Sahnun's *Mudawwana* (The Record), arguably the central text of Malikism of its time. The other was a commentary on a complementary text: Sahnun's lesser known opinions. Ibn Rushd's commentary was so successful that it replaced the existing version of the text, known as the *'Utbiyya*. Ibn Rushd's text and commentary thus supplanted the existing version, which consisted of an anthology of opinions and layers of commentaries by earlier authorities. The popularity of Ibn Rushd's updated commentary and rewriting meant that the original version and title ceased to be copied.[4] This process is typical of how medieval libraries and corpora replicated themselves, through a kind of organic transformation consisting of commentary, abridgment, and expostulation, well beyond simple and mechanical reproduction. It also points to how Ibn Rushd and several of his contemporaries brought about the theoretical elaboration of Malikism just mentioned. Ibn Rushd thus occupied a central position of prestige in the networks of learning and scholarship in the Peninsula, which was further enhanced by 'Ali's patronage by direct and public consultation and acknowledgment of authority in certain legal and religious matters. As students of Islamic law well know, while the production and compilation of these opinions is central to the substantive and theoretical elaboration of the law (questions and opinions were compiled for reference), *fatwā*s were not binding. The questioner (or *mustaftī*) had discretion in following the most convincing opinion and issuing a ruling. The vast majority of these responsa were formulated

---

4 On this point, see Ana Fernández Félix, *Cuestiones Legales del Islam Temprano: La 'Utbiyya y el Proceso de Formación de la Sociedad Islámica Andalusí, Estudios Árabes e Islamicos: Monografías* 6 (Madrid: Consejo Superior de Investigaciones Científicas, 2003).

for working judges. And 'Ali, as amir, held the ultimate power to decide on a course of action (when he himself asked a question). But his act of consultation bolstered the legal consultatory network across the Almoravid territories and lent legitimacy to his government's policies.

The two questions 'Ali directed to Ibn Rushd were the following. First, can the opinions and teachings of Ibn Bajja and his contemporaries and their theological ideas be heeded and trusted (what would later become associated with Ash'ari theology, a mainstream of Sunni theological thought)? And second, does the obligation of pilgrimage to Mecca remain valid and binding in conditions such as those befalling al-Andalus and the Maghrib, when there is general insecurity to person and property and great uncertainty and peril for the traveller in the lands to be crossed on the way east, as well as there being an existential threat to the lands of the Muslim west, especially al-Andalus, posed by non-Muslim powers (perhaps they would do better staying home to defend their lands)? Does this make the obligation to defend the Muslim community paramount or greater than the individual obligation to perform pilgrimage?

The first question involved doctrine, belief, and theology; the second concerned religious obligations, including the defence of the community over which 'Ali was sovereign (articulated in religious terms). Both are complex questions which have been dealt with in depth in recent scholarship. For our interests, a few general observations can be made, adding to our understanding of the social and institutional developments in the Maghrib under the Almoravids, and dispelling older entrenched notions about this history. One old view posited that the Almoravids were simply fanatical zealots. Another was that 'Ali was excessively pious and beholden of "the *faqīhs*" (the jurists or jurisprudents). These notions have separate sources and implications but play off a familiar trope of excessive and/or misguided dogmatic zeal. The point to be emphasized here is not to refute such tropes point by point, but to criticize them and provide a different framework in which to read such texts and episodes as these. In the framework developed in this book, we have posited that one of 'Ali's significant achievements was to oversee and promote the development of the legal network by patronizing (e.g., by funding the education of students) and appointing Maliki jurists as legal administrators and by fomenting communication between the Andalusi and Mahghribi networks. Far from being simply a zealot convinced of Almoravid dogma, these two questions demonstrate 'Ali's openness to learned opinion and his respect for the legal authority of Ibn Rushd. The bridge built by such gestures and practical correspondence was of great impact. Also noteworthy is that these questions point to an interesting dimension of Andalusi (and Maghribi) exceptionalism, in which their particular circumstances justify taking exceptional measures and formulating exceptional doctrines. This was indeed the case with the question of the recision or disestablishment of the pilgrimage (hajj) as an obligation, a question which recurred in the region (along with Ibn Rushd's influential opinion). These questions, moreover, point to a great upsurge in intellectual, spiritual, and religious activity, which the Almoravid state endeavoured to harness, not always successfully.

The vast majority of texts and questions generated by the consultative legal network sponsored by 'Ali, however, were not religious in nature and arguably more influential (than these two admittedly very interesting questions). They brought up a host of issues concerning commerce, property, legal procedure, legal education, criminal procedure, agricultural practice, and riparian arrangements. Which is to say that the generation of Maliki jurists who appeared under Almoravid sponsorship dealt with a wide variety of mundane and practical matters. And while offering a narrow window, they are telling and illustrative. Ibn Rushd, for example, was asked about resolving disputes in commercial transactions and currency exchanges, about lawful forms of gold exchange, the individuation of property (land), the handling and status of questionably procured property, about determining priority in water uses given to agriculture versus manufacture, and about the status of professional witnesses. He was also asked questions on religious matters, such as on ablution and apostasy (an intriguing case in which, tellingly, Ibn Rushd urges against rash action).

This juridical activity illustrates some key points: That later manuals of Islamic law were influenced by this formative period, which was more productive and intellectually and substantively generative than was previously thought, adding to the notion that these jurists influenced the formulation of a theoretically informed Malikism; that the areas of activity over which Islamic law had purview, in places such as al-Andalus and Ifriqiya, came under the purview of Islamic law in the Maghrib in this period; and that this occurred by the creation and generation of spaces where such activities took place. The most obvious such spaces were the markets of the cities founded and developed by the Almoravids, and all of the commercial infrastructure joining them to each other and to the countryside. The second obvious space is the literate community itself: the development of a generation of jurists necessitates teachers and schools of higher education and texts and shared curricula, which generated all kinds of questions, about which texts or authorities to rely on, as part of the educational process (the responsorial exchange—the *istiftā'* and *fatwā*—were central practices to this education even if at times fictive).[5]

* * *

This bureaucratic and administrative complexification resonated far beyond the borders of the state and was part of a larger story, in the Mediterranean and in the Sahara and beyond. As noted above, this period marked the beginning of the golden age of Saharan and trans-Saharan commerce, which developed a rich commercial network that depended

---

5 On juristic culture and the legal system in al-Andalus, see: Maribel Fierro, "Scholars, Jurists and the Legal System," in *The Routledge Handbook of Medieval Iberia*, edited by Fierro, 290–317. And for a more detailed description of the Maghribi context, see Gómez-Rivas, *Law and the Islamization of Morocco under the Almoravids.*

directly on the textual tools and social institutions developed under the Almoravids: the legal instruments used in Saharan commerce and long-distance trade entered the region, particularly in the larger western Saharan region, at this time. This gave rise to distinctive centres of literacy in the Sahara itself and, in the long run, was foundational for the rise of literate elites and state formation in the Sahel and Western Africa, where Islamic and Islamicate legal and administrative forms and structures would play a major role. Trans-Saharan connections with eastern North Africa, including Egypt, would prove equally influential, but the Almoravid episode and what it meant for the development of western trade routes and textual practices created the basis for later developments. The Mediterranean presents a more complicated picture, but a similar point can be made: Overall, the southern Mediterranean developed practices and instruments that would be used and adopted by merchants from the northern shores. Incidences of this process can be seen across the Mediterranean and into the Early Modern period. The Almoravids do not constitute a single source for such practices, but their emergence in the western Mediterranean as a major political and commercial player is contemporary with the growing flow of Western Mediterranean trade across a richer network. This trade, especially as it brought in Aragonese and Genoese traders, would flower a little later, but the legal and textual instruments and the commercial practices and institutions that made it possible owe a great deal to developments of the Almoravid period, when Ceuta became a major port and risk-sharing instruments of long distance trade became adopted by Arabic and Romance speaking merchants alike.

Table 1: Succession of Amirs in the Almoravid Dynasty (of the Banu Targut)

Yahya b. ʿUmar (b. Ibrahim b. Targut)	434–447/1042–1055
Abu Bakr b. ʿUmar	447–480/1055–1087
Yusuf b. Tashfin (b. Ibrahim b. Targut)	480–500/1087–1106
ʿAli b. Yusuf	500–537/1106–1143
Tashfin b. ʿAli	537–539/1143–1145
Ibrahim b. Tashfin	539/1145
Ishaq b. ʿAli	539–541/1145–1147

Chapter 5

The Mahdis

The latter half of 'Ali's rule witnessed a marked increase in political opposition, perhaps most prominently of a messianic nature. A wide-ranging environment of spiritual speculation and creativity provided the social context for these. The most famous of these messianic movements would found the ensuing dynasty, often read as part of a separate history. The fact is, however, that the Almoravid Maghrib, as presided over by 'Ali b. Yusuf, was where the Almohad mahdist movement had its origins, roots, and causes, even if it came as a violent reaction to what was there.

Ibn Tumart

In a scene redolent with meaning (likely too literary to be true), Muhammad b. Tumart (d. 524/1130) a powerfully charismatic itinerant preacher at the time, arrived in Marrakesh and began berating the Almoravids for their corruption. "He overturned wine and smashed musical instruments" and confronted 'Ali, the *Amīr al-Muslimīn* himself, and refused to recognize him, for, among other things, wearing a veil in the Lamtuna style (being one of the *mulaththamūn*, one of the "veiled ones," as Almoravids were referred to in some of the literature).[1] "I only see veiled women here," he said and called

---

[1] The head covering, presumably similar to what the Touareg wear, is called a *lithām*.

on 'Ali to repent and reform: "The caliphate does not belong to you but to God."[2] Ibn Tumart's intervention turned into a disputation with the 'ulama' present and whom Ibn Tumart reportedly accused of over-literal interpretations of scripture (such as picturing God in corporal form). Some days later, Ibn Tumart was said to confront 'Ali's sister, for lacking modesty as she was riding a horse, going unveiled. He slapped the haunch of the horse, which then threw her to the ground. Ibn Tumart was summoned to court where he was questioned. This turned again into a debate in which Ibn Tumart roundly defeated his interlocutors in argumentation about law, theology, and ethics. The story would seem to convey that the preacher enjoyed great popularity and support (unavailable to the other such critics of the regime) especially if its conclusion is true: Malik b. Wuhayb, Maliki jurist and senior advisor to 'Ali, recognizing the danger posed by this supposedly simple, itinerant preacher, advised that he be imprisoned on the spot. Another advisor, however, Yintan b. 'Umar (a Lamtuni vizier and troop commander), urged that the preacher, so wise in matters of religion, be allowed to go about his business. 'Ali chose to banish Ibn Tumart who turned to preaching and organizing the Masmuda in the mountains south of Marrakesh and would re-emerge as a messianic mahdi figure.

Ibn Tumart was a Masmuda Berber from the Hargha tribe. He grew up in the village of Igliz, in the Sus Valley (where Ibn Yasin's teacher had his Dar al-Murabitin). The Masmuda were one of the largest groups that the Lamtuna had encountered as they conquered and unified the Maghrib, concentrated in the Middle and High Atlas and surrounding valleys. Several Masmuda groups recognized the Lamtuna leadership of the Almoravid state, but were rarely, if ever, brought into the higher echelons of administration. Over the long run, this lack of assimilation would provide fertile grounds for resentment, which Ibn Tumart would strive to articulate and promote. Young Muhammad b. Tumart was devout and had a calling for religious learning, which he pursued through

---

2 Messier, *The Almoravids*, 141.

travel (following a well-established Islamic pattern, to meet other pious and wise personalities and learn from them). It is certain he travelled throughout the Maghrib, but he is said to have travelled far and wide, to al-Andalus and to the East (the Mashriq), to Arabia and Baghdad. The veracity of these accounts is unlikely, but again, their existence as literary artifacts is important. As the founder of a successful messianic movement and state, the biography of Ibn Tumart is shrouded in legend, typical of the hagiographic genre of heroic founder. The narrative sheds light on the development of the religious culture of the Maghrib, on what issues and symbols were meaningful and contested. A prime example is the fiercely contested reception of al-Ghazali's work and thought in the Maghrib and al-Andalus, which coincided with the late Almoravid and early Almohad periods. One of the significant episodes in the story of Ibn Tumart's travels to the East seeks to establish a direct relationship with al-Ghazali, whom Ibn Tumart is said to have met and studied under, and thus, on his return to the Maghrib, to represent as emissary and embodiment of the epochal change and spiritual revival al-Ghazali began to symbolize. Ibn Tumart's followers and hagiographers drew from a spiritual culture that entertained ideas of spiritual revival. They sought to associate Ibn Tumart and al-Ghazali, a figure that was emerging as one of the principal figures in the new Islamic spirituality of the late fifth/eleventh and early sixth/twelfth centuries and who, as we have seen, also had some positive reception among Almoravid and Maliki 'ulama' (although not uncontested).[3] The social and spiritual effervescence of the second half of 'Ali's reign alarmed the administrative class—both military and religious—eliciting measures of control, including co-optation, but also suppression and elimination.

---

3 On Ibn Tumart and al-Ghazali, see Frank Griffel, "Ibn Tūmart's Rational Proof for God's Existence and His Unity, and His Connection to the Niẓāmiyya *madrasa* in Bagdad," in *Los Almohades*, ed. Cressier, Fierro, and Molina, 2:753–813.

The most famous act of suppression consisted of a series of, now infamous, book burnings, specifically of al-Ghazali's *Iḥyā'*, the first of which took place before Ibn Tumart's arrival on the scene and the most prevalent of which took place in al-Andalus (notably in the port of Almería). These appear to have been instigated by prominent members of the Andalusi 'ulama', from Córdoba, Seville, and Almería. One of the figures associated with the book burnings, Ibn Hamdin, was a member of a distinguished family of Córdoban jurists. They appear to have been threatened by something in al-Ghazali's work or by a way in which it was being employed locally. Whatever the exact reading, it appears to have involved a struggle over social and spiritual authority in the community, between the Maliki 'ulama' (with their enhanced authority under the Almoravid state) and the alternative expressions from charismatic figures associated with mysticism, Sufism, messianism, and popular piety and preaching. Ibn Tumart entered the scene as the embodiment of the latter. He had spent some well-documented time in Tunis and Algeria, where he made a life-long alliance with 'Abd al-Mu'min, who would later become critical for the success of the movement. He then travelled west preaching piety, purity, and religious reform, from to town, as he returned to his homeland where he would clash with the highest of Almoravid authorities.

Fertile Almoravid Ground for the Reception of Ibn Tumart

The rise of such a figure needs fertile ground for its successful reception. This had been produced by the new state and its deeper integration of the countryside. The stability of government under the Almoravids rested, to a great extent, on local agents. Power under Yusuf and 'Ali depended on a complex network of local administration. In certain places, and in much of the Maghrib especially, this entailed the development of new forms and agents of local authority and the empowerment of existing offices and agents. Musa b. Hammad, for example, provides a good model of the kind of individual belonging to this new administrative class. He was the chief qadi (judge) of Marrakesh (a relatively new jurisdiction). He was a local, and thus a representative of the new generation of literate administrators. He penned the formal question to Ibn Rushd (mentioned above) about an accusation of apostasy that took place in Marrakesh in the first quarter of the fifth/twelfth century. He summarized the case for Ibn Rushd, underscoring what he thought were the most relevant points of law: a Latin Christian (a Catalan mercenary perhaps?) who lived in Marrakesh, had publicly professed Islam. Later, however, he was accused of reverting. The accused's living quarters were inspected, producing a set of suspicious objects: a lectern, a bible, and some eucharistic hosts. Musa asked Ibn Rushd what should be done with the accused, with an emphasis on procedure. In the formal answer (fatwā) Ibn Rushd walked the consulting jurist through the aspects he thought relevant about the case: No one knew for sure that these objects belonged to the accused or that they, in fact, positively signalled a practising Christian. The accused should be given the chance to explain himself, and if he maintained that he was indeed apostatizing, he should be granted the opportunity to reflect and correct himself.

The case is interesting for a variety of reasons: For one, it shows that there were Christians living in Marrakesh and that the Almoravid government likely employed them (which we know from other later sources). It also would seem to show that intrigue was easily sparked by accusations of infidelity or unbelief and that local figures of judicial and religious authority intervened to negotiate the potential conflict. These in turn had recourse to other figures of authority through the network of consultation (in this case Marrakesh communicating with Córdoba). In fact, Musa is attested to elsewhere in the juridical consultative literature produced by this network. In one instance he gave his legal opinion for a case on judicial review and water law, presided over by Qadi 'Iyad in Ceuta (and whom we will meet in next chapter). These consultations and cases bear evidence for the success of the network and its functional presence in judicial administration. The social authority of this network and establishment rested on the embodiment of justice and its spiritual knowledge in the community; it traced its origins back to the Prophet Muhammad and to his community in Medina, which was the point of pride of Maliki law and practice: that its founder had learned and transmitted everything he knew, including words as well as practice, from the community that had lived with the Prophet (thus the importance in Malikism of the concept of "The Practice of the People of Medina" or ʿamal ahl al-Madīna). Which is to say that the Maliki ʿulamaʾ claimed to embody the Prophet and his companions, to be living representatives and thus to capture the charisma of the Prophet and the companions for latter day Muslims (to put it in Weberian terms).[4]

The notion of charisma as the basis of social authority is particularly useful here since it expresses a sense of authority imbued with a force more attractive and affectively powerful than the practical, functional, and bureaucratic force I have been emphasizing. The fact that new administrative agents could combine these powers (spiritual, charismatic, and practical), however, is what made them effective to begin with. This helps us understand a phenomenon of the latter half of the Almoravid era, which witnessed the emergence of a series of alternative sources of social authority, which emerged as a backlash from groups on the margins and from those coming into increasing contact with the agents of the administration and associated state spaces. A rich variety of new actors appeared as a result, and they articulated their challenge or opposition in terms that addressed the spiritual, religious, and moral claims of the Almoravid military tribal core and the community of religious scholars and jurists they had empowered and relied on.

The situation in al-Andalus was similar. But because of its longer and richer traditions of city and state, challenges and alternatives took on different and more varied forms. The similarity is important to highlight, however, because the traditional narrative distorts important elements of the reception

---

4 Albarrán Iruela, *Veneración y polémica*.

and response to the Almoravid intervention in al-Andalus. This narrative portrayed the Almoravids strictly as a religiously motivated force that, because of its backwardness and unsophistication (not to mention its resolutely Berber ethnic identity and Saharan foreignness) was resisted, challenged, and despised by Andalusis across the board. As we have seen, this was far from the case. 'Abd Allah b. Buluggin tells us as much when he describes how his carefully organized defences (a chain of fortresses) melted away as the troops and leadership of these defected. 'Abd Allah complains that defending the kingdom had been doomed because of the widespread popularity of Yusuf, his policies, values, and what he appeared to symbolize. The Almoravids were an unstoppable force in al-Andalus, largely because they enjoyed widespread support among the population and among key elements of the religious and bureaucratic class. Ibn Rushd al-Jadd's dedicated contribution to the administration of justice illustrates this support and popularity among established elite families of the old Umayyad capital. Ibn Rushd, moreover, was not alone nor was he the single most eminent of the Andalusi 'ulama' to join forces with the Almoravids. There are numerous other examples. One figure of note was Abu Bakr b. al-'Arabi, who originally left Seville with his father on pilgrimage, because of the turmoil associated with the Almoravid conquest, but returned seven years later—his father having died during the journey—after expending a great deal of effort to secure precious letters of support for Yusuf and his cause from the 'Abbasid caliph in Baghdad and from Abu Hamid al-Ghazali himself, whose influence would become highly contested by anti- and pro-Almoravid factions. While disruption among the ruling and religious elites did occur as a result of the Almoravid conquest, a family such as Abu Bakr b. al-'Arabi's could realign itself with the regime, because some of their values were significantly in alignment. These values could be construed as "religious," but they also touched on associated "secular" notions of fairness and justice for a wider section of society: That the rule of law and God represented by the Shari'a and the 'ulama' could and did often speak for a more popular social and economic legitimacy and justice. It is not surprising to find that the clearest formulation in al-Andalus of political legitimacy under the sultanic form of government (in which the 'ulama' play this central role) was advanced by a judge in Almoravid Seville. In his *Risalālat al-Qaḍā' wa'l-ḥisba* (Treatise on the Jurisdictions of Qadi and Market Inspector), Ibn 'Abdun describes the centrality of the Muslim judge in governing the community. The image he puts forth of the Almoravids contains just the right balance of fear and respect and a desire to keep them circumscribed to a specific role while granting the 'ulama' a central role in governing day-to-day functions in the community.

Resistance to Almoravid Presence in al-Andalus

This evident popularity notwithstanding, there were significant forms of resistance to the Almoravid presence in al-Andalus from the very beginning. Some of these were the typical form of recurrent and endemic resistance that the Umayyads had faced. Others were specific to the circumstances, which pitted a region with a long tradition of autonomous state structures against an upstart administration from a region and ethnic group with little prestige or state traditions of their own. The fragmentation of the Ta'ifas with its multiple and competing centres of power had shaped the landscape the Almoravids would encounter. The regional political elites associated with the Ta'ifa governments posed one form of vocal resistance and dissatisfaction. One example of such a voice can be found in the poetry of Ibn Quzman, a Ta'ifa court poet and greatest exponent of one of al-Andalus's characteristic and original literary forms: the *zajal*. This was a rowdy and colloquial kind of poetry and song, in which the Almoravids and their Andalusi allies are routinely mocked and comically represented.[5] These kinds of voices, associated with the notions of Andalusi autonomy and its

---

5 See a poem of this type by Abu Ja'far in Messier, *The Almoravids*, 127.

cultural superiority, appears recurrently in the literary and historiographical tradition of Almoravid al-Andalus; their origins traced back to the cultural production of the Taʾifa courts, which played host to debates framed in terms of superior and lesser groups, often pitting Arabs against Berbers (the latter being blamed, among other things, for the collapse of Umayyad and Arab rule in al-Andalus). Critiques of Almoravid rule echo the themes and sentiments of the ethnic rivalry literature of classical Arabic literature. But this kind of ethnically-based anti-Berber opposition (often associated with political and cultural elites) wasn't the only form to be expressed. A distinctly religious challenge was also voiced in a variety of forms, associated with figures who would become important (indeed foundational) in the history of mysticism and Sufism in the Islamic West. The Almoravid response to these challenges, moreover, indicates that they were taken very seriously by Almoravid officials on both sides of the Mediterranean.

The most important Sufi of the period, Ibn al-ʿArif, appears not to have been directly engaged in political agitation or rebellion. But the messianism of some of his associates and his own central role in the emergence of the mystical traditions points not only to the impact of the movement but to its creative and disruptive spiritual and social power. One intriguing associate, Ibn Barrajan, composed a tract in the tradition of the beautiful names of God and was acclaimed in a number of mosques in the region outside Seville as a regional spiritual leader, as imam, implying a kind of open religio-political rebellion (since, in this context, the imam was the singular leader of the community, political and spiritual). He was summoned to Marrakesh to never return.[6] Further west in southern Portugal, another messianic figure—also personally connected to Ibn al-ʿArif—appears also to have been clearly involved in outright political rebellion. Abu al-Qasim Ahmad b. al-Husayn b. Qasi was born into a family of Christian heritage in Shilb (Silves) in southwestern Portugal. Little is known about Ibn

---

6 Casewit, *The Mystics of al-Andalus.*

Qasi's early life. He had held the job of financial inspector or customs collector (*mushrif*) in his town before experiencing a spiritual awakening that compelled him to give away his possessions and wander across al-Andalus as an ascetic and spiritual seeker. He met Ibn al-'Arif (who would also be summoned to Marrakesh, but, unlike Ibn Barrajan, released and allowed to return) before returning to Jilla, a town outside Shilb, where he founded his own spiritual refuge (or *rābiṭa*) with a group of devotees. In the turbulent 530s/1140s, Ibn Qasi recast himself as a mahdi (a messianic redeemer) with the support of local notables and forces. His career as messianic rebel was short-lived and violent. He had to reckon with greater powers coming out of the Maghrib and was forced to renounce his spiritual claim. But he stands as a distinctive figure of the late Almoravid political and religious landscape: characteristic of the forms of local power emerging to challenge the Almoravid state. This was both characteristic of a weakening state and of a culture burgeoning with new ideas and social forces. Many of these ideas and figures have traditionally been associated with Sufism, and it appears clear that the Almoravid period was foundational for Sufism in the Islamic West. But it is also evident that a variety of political, spiritual, and religious movements were distinct from the traditions normally associated with Sufism. Ibn Qasi's own extant work, for example, unlike Ibn Barrajan's *Sharḥ asmā' Allah al-ḥuṣna* (Commentary on the Beautiful Names of God, a genre meditating on God's qualities that has a long association with Sufism), is more aligned with the apocalyptic and millenarian traditions of Isma'ilism—that is, with themes of cyclical historical development, messianic expectation, and predictions of coming redemption. While sometimes associated with mysticism, these themes and ideas have their own distinct and powerful social and political presence. They were also very popular in al-Andalus, and perhaps even more so in the Maghrib, where, the greatest challenge to the Almoravids emerged, as we have seen, in the figure of this itinerant preacher, sharing several of these messianic and millenarian characteristics.

The Almohads

The rise of Ibn Tumart's movement—which came to be known as that of the Almohads (in Arabic: *al-Muwaḥḥidūn*, those who proclaim the unity of God) and out of which another imperial state would emerge—exhibits significant structural and political parallels to that of the Almoravids, for which the two movements or dynasties have often been lumped together: a new Maghribi tribal coalition galvanized by a religious movement, led by a charismatic figure, spurring a reformist movement that turned to conquest. Ibn Tumart's movement seems to calque the rise of the Almoravids. On the other hand, Ibn Tumart positioned himself very clearly as a detractor of the Almoravid platform. And what developed from his and his followers' teachings was a movement with a theology nearly opposite to that of the Almoravids. Their entire symbology aimed at countering the basis of Almoravid legitimacy (especially in the Maghrib). Bolstered by his anti-Almoravid critique, Ibn Tumart would lead the single greatest challenge to the Almoravid state, a challenge that would prove overwhelming (even if not in Ibn Tumart's own life-time). The grounds for mounting this opposition was based on a religious culture much like that which gave rise to Ibn Qasi and Ibn Barrajan, but in a region riper with messianic expectation (if the strength and success of the movement is anything to go by). And while Ibn Tumart's status as messianic figure would—as with other such movements—be pared down with time to something less unorthodox, his legacy would prove influential for generations.[7]

To restate: The Almohad movement was a continuation of the process of state building initiated by the Almoravids. We can think of it as a second wave in the process we have been investigating here, involving a large scale development of state institutions, spaces and urban development. They

7 Serrano, "¿Por qué llamaron los Almohades antropomorfistas a los Almorávides?," in *Los Almohades*, ed. Cressier, Fierro, and Molina, 2:815–47.

built on the foundations laid by the Almoravids and pursued similar broad strategies of legitimation, while introducing new variations and ideas in areas where the Almoravid state had exhibited structural weaknesses. On the other hand, and because they emerged as a challenge and reaction, the substance and character of the movements were very different. The theology and political agenda of the Almohads positioned themselves in opposition to the Almoravids. Almohad propaganda and historical writing, moreover, left a grossly distorted view of Almoravid theology, ideology, and practice; these writings often expressed more about the Almohads and their positioning than about the Almoravids' practices and beliefs. Almohad chroniclers depicted their Almoravids predecessors as enslaved to legalistic detail and spiritually shallow, even empty; as unjust, tyrannical, and culturally other, including in their performance of gender (reversing gender roles, with effeminate men and masculine women).[8] We glimpse from this competition and enmity between the successive movements and imperial chapters the evolving character of the relationship between key constituencies and forces: religious belief, charismatic religious figures, the countryside, the growing urban spaces, the 'ulama' (the class of literate specialists), and the tribal federations that formed the backbone of real military power.

Ibn Tumart's support among the Masmuda in the High Atlas would gradually consume the energy of the Almoravid army in a decade-long guerrilla campaign that would eventually conquer Marrakesh and bring down the state. Ibn Tumart built a small *ribāṭ* in his village where he surrounded himself with his followers. He was proclaimed mahdi (redeemer of the religion) in 515/1121. 'Ali sent waves of unsuccessful campaigns against the growing movement of the Almohads who ensconced themselves in a mountain redoubt (and first capital) in Tinmal. For a long time, the Almohads were unable to face and defeat the Almoravids in open battle (not in 'Ali's lifetime at least). The Almohads successfully repelled a siege

---

8 Bennison, *Almoravid and Almohad Empires*, 65.

in 524/1130, after which Ibn Tumart died, and the leadership of the movement passed to 'Abd Al-Mu'min, who would go on to conquer Marrakesh–although not for another seventeen years–and proclaim himself caliph, as he and his successors styled themselves: Caliphs of God and successors of the Mahdi Ibn Tumart, a concept they incorporated into their central doctrine of faith: There is no God but God, Muhammad is the Messenger of God and Ibn Tumart is the Mahdi of God. The Mu'minid Almohad dynasty would rule from Marrakesh for a long century.

The Almoravid Military

Throughout 'Ali's reign, he and his army were kept busy with regular campaigns, local rebellions, and complex and dynamic borderlands in Spain, the Maghrib, and the Sahara. A detailed chronicle of the military history of the end of 'Ali's reign, including the response to the Almohad uprising, would easily overwhelm this book. For the sake of brevity and synthesis, I will try to characterize the evolution of 'Ali's military campaigns as a whole and what this meant for Almoravid politics and society. The first ten or fifteen years of 'Ali's reign were marked by a continuation of Yusuf's policies and by some success in terms of expansion and consolidation along the Iberian frontier, which was active across its wide expanse and throughout this period. The abilities of the Christian kingdoms of the north of the Peninsula to maintain cohesion and focus enterprising martial energy towards al-Andalus (attracting intermittent but powerful support from beyond the Pyrenees, often in the form of the support from French lords) meant that the threat along the Iberian frontier was ever-present. This was counterbalanced by the fact that one of the main preoccupations of the Christian kings of Iberia was to fend off attacks from their co-religionist neighbours. As we have seen, Castile's rise to prominence, consolidating the territories of Castile–Leon and the city of Toledo, had prompted the Almoravid incursion. Subsequent warfare along the frontier, around Valencia and Zaragoza, was often promoted and conditioned by Castile's influence. This subsided with Alfonso's death in 503/1109. The major force that emerged to replace Castile was the Kingdom of Aragon, under Alfonso I, known as *el Batallador*, an aggressive and enterprising neighbour who led a series of deep and destructive raids across al-Andalus in the 510s/1120s.

On the whole, the Almoravids maintained a strong and competent military presence in al-Andalus. There were no conclusive, large scale victories of Christians over Muslims or vice-versa. Among other reasons, this is because routine military politics and preoccupations did not involve Christian-Muslim conflict—the kind of universal, large scale civilizational conflict between the religions that is often imagined or invoked—but much more local and regional conflict which can be described as internecine. The Christian-Muslim frontier, moreover, was complex and always involved interreligious alliances and acknowledgements. Crusading ideology could be invoked but did not characterize routine conflicts and campaigning. An important inflection point did occur, however, and involved a realignment of alliances (with clear negative impact on Almoravid al-Andalus), and this conditioned the second half of 'Ali's reign and resulting in a growing sense of pressure from the north: This was the fall of Zaragoza to Aragon in 511/1118, a denouement which took place through defection motivated by internal politics, but which, in the end, delivered another prize Muslim city on the scale of Toledo—this time to the kingdom of Aragon. Overnight, Aragon's population doubled. And this all (the fall of Toledo and Zaragoza) happened before there existed any ability to mount large scale attacks and invasions of Muslim territories. The "fall" of these two cities considerably affected the dynamics of the frontier by delivering wealthy concentrations of populations, with their agrarian hinterlands, to Castile and Aragon, greatly increasing their size and wealth. Neither was the result of major military campaigns.

Two further points bear emphasizing in the general evolution of the Almoravid military: One was that it had succeeded by relying on a coherent leadership, including a small number of trusted and competent leaders, who became difficult to replace. From the 510s/1120s a series of key figures began to pass away without suitable replacement, leaving a vacuum in the leadership. The second regards the evolution of the makeup of the fighting force as a whole. What began as a tribal and clan-based invading force, with time was forced to evolve to include professional and mercenary troops, naturally requiring an evolution of the fiscal structure that supported the military, including the imposition of taxes, undermining Almoravid legitimacy in the later years of the empire. This Khaldunian evolution, in which an ethnically or tribally cohesive conquering group begins to assimilate and requires supplementation and creation of new military forces, was a recurrent problem that dynasties and empires like the Almoravids had to deal with. The Almohads would create large contingents of paid and recruited regiments (more diversely and successfully). As noted, the Almoravid military and governing structure was characterized by reliance on the specific groups that formed the original confederation. Nevertheless, the Almoravids did recruit mercenary troops and relied on them, and especially heavily in their final struggles for survival. Their inability to replenish troops at all levels, moreover, appears to have been exacerbated by the gradual blockade that the Almohad movement managed to impose on the Almoravid state between the state's principal cities and its Saharan homeland in the south. (It can be described as "Khaldunian," because of Ibn Khaldun (d. 808/1406), the great Maghribi historian who developed a theory of political and social evolution—a theory of the cyclical evolution of the state—in which a tribal group or federation bringing new blood gradually loses cohesion and charisma and needs replacement by another; this theory was largely informed by the Almoravid, Almohad, and Marinid political experiences.)

The End of the Almoravid State

The downfall of the Almoravid state had its epicentre in the Maghrib, where its core military structure and its fiscal bases were located. Originally centred on the Western-Saharan commercial routes, these were gradually supplanted by eastern connections, supported by alliances with groups like the Banu Masufa, a tribal group from which the influential Banu Ghaniya family came. These new alliances and additions to the leadership helped offset some of the military and commercial insufficiencies, but not sufficiently to stem the decline. An Almohad shadow state with its own tribal federation and network of allied villages and groups gradually developed over the last decade of Almoravid rule, extending its presence across the western Maghrib and into al-Andalus, where they were increasingly recognized as legitimate powers-that-be (and the Almoravid state fractured as local actors moved to reassert their autonomy). After a major setback in al-Andalus, 'Ali had replaced his brother Tamim as governor of al-Andalus with his son Tashfin b. 'Ali, where the latter led a series of campaigns before returning to the Maghrib where he campaigned tirelessly against the Almohads along the growing Almohad-Almoravid divide. Tashfin became his father's right-hand man and designated successor. He was one of the last able military leaders of the empire. His own principal auxiliary commander was a Catalan mercenary known as Reverter. Together they fought a dogged last-ditch defence of the empire, for a decade.

'Ali b. Yusuf b. Tashfin died in 537/1142 after thirty-six years of rule. News of his death reached Tashfin who then took measures to secure recognition of his succession from the key constituencies. It is fair to say, however, that a successful succession from 'Ali to Tashfin never fully materialized and that Tashfin inherited an empire in crisis, in danger of imminent collapse. A substantial portion of the Almoravid political community, cognizant of the precarious situation of the empire, failed or refused to recognize the new sovereign, waiting for indications of new alliances and shapes yet to form. This was the exact moment when Ibn Qasi's rebellion reached its full flower in al-Andalus, and when he sought an alliance with the Almohads, seeing common cause and affinity. But, such was the latter's strength by now that, upon visiting the Maghrib for an audience with ʿAbd al-Muʾmin, Ibn Qasi had to walk back his pretensions. He is said to have apologized with the phrase: "I was the false dawn before the true dawn of Ibn Tumart." Tashfin did manage to secure his position within the Almoravid core, but lost a great number of tributary groups and communities. ʿAbd al-Muʾmin, by contrast, proceeded from strength to strength, consolidating his political position and gathering alliances, tribute, and recognition as local leader and as leader of the Umma in the West, under a newly articulated formula of legitimacy (Caliph of the Almohad Empire and successor of the Mahdi Ibn Tumart). Reverter, the Almoravid Catalan mercenary, perished in battle along with many of his troops just around the time when the Almohads became, for the first time, capable of confronting the Almoravids in open battle. And so Tashfin b. ʿAli would meet his end shortly after, on the battle field, in 539/1145.[9] His reign had been but a desperate three-year battle to shore up the collapsing state. And with his demise, as perhaps the last competent and unifying Almoravid military commander, little hope remained for the empire to hold.

There followed two short-lived successors, both minors, ruling for a few months each, before ʿAbd al-Muʾmin felt ready to take Marrakesh by force. After a long siege and a series of pitched battles,[10] the Almohads entered the city. ʿAbd al-Muʾmin remained outside the walls and would not enter until the mosques—or their mihrabs rather—were corrected to their proper orientation (in many cases involving razing the structure).[11] Ishaq b. ʿAli b. Yusuf, the last of the Almoravid amirs, hid in his palace until he was caught. He tried to declare that he was blameless of the faults of his predecessors and should not pay for their mistakes, for which ʿAbd al-Muʾmin ordered him to be beheaded. With the capitula-

9 Bennison, *Almoravid and Almohad Empires*, 59.

10 Messier, *The Almoravids*, 168.

11 On the Almoravid and Almohad mosques and the change of *qibla*, see Stockstill, "A Tale of Two Mosques."

tion of the Almoravid capital, many of the symbols of state were assiduously erased. Dome decorations were plastered over, mosques razed on the pretext of their dis-orientation. And equally dramatically, the Maliki establishment—that is, the network of 'ulama' that served as the administrative and legal network of the empire—was marked by Almohad policy for being done away with and replaced. 'Abd al-Mu'min was happy to build on the foundations laid by the Almoravids as long as these were invisible. And much Almoravid history and material legacy was obliterated in this way. Some fundamental legacies would remain indelible along with further flung offshoots that would irksomely persist throughout Almohad rule.

Chapter 6

The Qadi and the Rebel

The mahdist movement of the Almohads would overwhelm the Almoravid state, but many of the innovations brought about under Almoravid rule would stick tenaciously in the long term. Loyalty to the institutions it had fostered and even to the dynasty itself, in spite of its collapse, was dogged, lasting in some places into the late Almohad period. The Almoravid institutional and cultural imprint would last even longer, providing the foundation for several of the characteristic intellectual, religious, and cultural traditions of the Far Maghrib.

Qadi ʿIyad

ʿIyad b. Musa was born in 476/1083 into a scholarly family in the port city of Ceuta, the same city where ʿAli b. Yusuf was born.[1] Ceuta grew into the Maghrib's most important port, and ʿIyad was in no small way affected and shaped by this growth and by the flow of people through his city. He studied with the some of the best teachers the city had to offer and met travelling scholars, of which there were many on account of Ceuta's location. ʿIyad was a prominent student of law when ʿAli b. Yusuf, as part of his effort to develop the administrative expertise of the empire, sponsored ʿIyad's study trip to al-Andalus. There he would meet and learn from the nota-

---

I ʿIyad's family claimed Yemeni origins.

ble Maliki scholars of Córdoba, Seville, and the other cities of the Peninsula. Unlike the likely fictive voyages to al-Andalus of Ibn Yasin and Ibn Tumart, 'Iyad's trip is well documented. He even wrote a compendium of biographies of the scholars he met there (his *al-Ghunya*, The Riches). And once returned to Ceuta, where he would eventually rise to chief judge, Qadi 'Iyad produced a voluminous correspondence with the best-known jurists of al-Andalus, many of which he had met in person. This correspondence, which consisted of formal legal consultations (or questions and opinions in answer to legal questions) was later compiled by his son.[2] Some of these question-and-answer texts feature prominently in the great ninth/fifteenth-century *fatwā* compendium by al-Wansharisi, where 'Iyad is one of the single most cited authors (albeit more as a source of questions than opinions). He corresponded frequently with Ibn Rushd al-Jadd as well as with lesser known jurists of al-Andalus and the Maghrib, including the above-mentioned chief judge of Marrakesh, Musa b. Hammad. The compilation provides a rich portrait of juristic and economic activity, shedding light on the nuts and bolts of commercial and institutional development, on the complexification of the Almoravid Maghrib as a result of its political unification and commercial growth. Al-Wansharisi's compendium is one text in which we encounter the first generation of Far Maghribi Maliki jurists (of which 'Iyad was the most prominent member). Another is 'Iyad's the *Tartib al-Madārik* (The Arrangement of the Faculties), the first Far Maghribi biographical dictionary of the Maliki school, which traces a significant dimension of institutional development, being composed and compiled from a Maghribi perspective, connecting the Maghribi scholarly establishment with that of al-Andalus, with Qayrawan and Ifriqiya, with the Malikis of Cairo, and, of course, with the founding tradition of Medina.

    'Iyad wrote another work of enduring fame and popularity, the *Shifā'* (The Healing), a work on the qualities and char-

---

2 Serrano, "Legal Practice in an Andalusī-Maghribī Source from the Twelfth Century CE."

acter of the Prophet Muhammad. This work, which survives in hundreds of manuscripts, while on the surface simply a work of piety on a subject quite naturally central to the religious tradition, can also be understood very much as a product of its time and place. It argues in its own subtle way for the authority and centrality of the representatives of the Maliki school as the guardians and keepers of the Prophet's example, representatives and true heirs of his spiritual light and charisma;[3] the composition of the *Shifā'* coincides with the formulation of sultanic government and its particular balance of power, in which the fully consolidated Sunni schools institutionalized the spiritual authority and charisma of the Prophetic tradition and channelled it into the administration of justice, lending legitimacy to the government that sponsored it. For this and the aforementioned works, 'Iyad is remembered as a towering and founding figure of the religious establishment in the Maghrib, as a paragon of the Almoravid period, and as a conduit of Andalusi spiritual traditions to the Maghrib. It is not surprising that al-Maqqari, the Arab historian whose writings and vision were most instrumental in shaping the long view of Andalusi history, centred the second of his two great works of history on 'Iyad, *Azhār al-Riyāḍ fī Akhbār 'Iyāḍ* (The Most Radiant of the Gardens in the Story of 'Iyad). The other, and more famous, one is centred on Ibn al-Khatib. We can think of these as something like "the Age of Ibn al-Khatib" and "the Age of 'Iyad." Such was the sense of 'Iyad's influence in the late medieval and early modern Maghrib, where he is most revered (he is one of the seven saints of Marrakesh and name-sake of its modern university).

'Iyad's career and life story demonstrates (to its very end) a deep connection and commitment to the Almoravid cause. After having his studies subsidized by Almoravid patronage, 'Iyad served on the city's judiciary (after graduating by taking part in a public debate on Sahnun), starting with the *shūra* (consultation) council he rose through the ranks to chief judge, a position to which he was appointed by 'Ali in

---

3 Albarrán Iruela, *Veneración y polémica*, 27, 161.

515/1121 and where he served longest. Latter in his career he was appointed (promoted perhaps) to serve as chief judge of Granada, in the year 531/1136. He did not last long in this post, however, since he soon clashed with the interests and customs of influential locals (over whom he is said to have judged too harshly). 'Iyad was appointed to the chief judge-ship of Ceuta for a second spell in 539–543/1145–1148. As the empire crumbled around him, and the Almoravid cities of the Maghrib began to fall to the new order, 'Iyad and his city and region had held fast for longer than many of the areas further south. 'Iyad crossed to Algeciras to request that Yahya b. 'Ali b. Ghaniya, the Almoravid governor of al-Andalus, reinforce Ceuta's defences. The governor complied, and sent the fugitive Almoravid prince, another Yahya: Yahya b. Abi Bakr al-Sahrawiyya, as reinforcements.[4] This Yahya al-Sahrawiyya mounted a last stand against the armies of 'Abd al-Mu'min, by gathering available troops in Tangier and leading a series of campaigns to defend the northern cities. 'Iyad stood with al-Sahrawiyya, even when the latter was forced to retreat south (in an attempt to regroup), and 'Iyad was left, as deputized leader of the city of Ceuta and resisted a months-long siege until it became patent that capitulation would be in the city's best interest. 'Iyad negotiated terms and surrendered himself and his city in 543/1148. Like his Ta'ifa predecessors, 'Iyad was taken as vanquished rebel to face his fate in Marrakesh. The Almohad leadership showed mercy on 'Iyad, exiling him to Tadla, a town in the vicinity of Marrakesh where 'Iyad saw out the rest of his days. But because of the widespread and enduring fame 'Iyad would achieve as author of the *Shifā'* (and as founding figure of Malikism in the Maghrib), biographical accounts in later and distant sources pepper his biography with new details; tellingly, symbolic elements (apocryphal and fantastical) encode elements of the struggle over spiritual authority between the legal establishment and the alternative forms: They accuse 'Iyad of burning al-Ghazali's famous book, the *Iḥyā' 'ulūm al-dīn* (The Revival of the

---

4 Bennison, *Almoravid and Almohad Empires*, 72.

Religious Sciences). He is said to have died in prison because of a curse uttered by al-Ghazali himself. Others say he fought alongside Almohad armies in latter battles. All are (likely and to my knowledge) factually inaccurate, but eloquently express the struggle over defining and owning 'Iyad's legacy.[5] The recurrent appearance of al-Ghazali also points to a process that transcended the Maghrib and was felt in other corners of an expanding Muslim World: a contest between institutionalized spiritual discourse and powerful lay and non-establishment spiritual figures and social movements, the best known of which gave rise to the Sufi orders that became regular and widespread from the sixth/twelfth century.

In the end, 'Iyad's legacy was indeed reconciled with these alternative currents, but gradually and not without contestation, and certainly not during the first half of the Almohad empire, when the new state embarked on a radical and ambitious agenda to articulate a new Islamic theology and rewrite the law, whole-sale (based on that new theology and religio-political authority).[6] The Almohad leader, assuming the titles of Caliph and successor of the Imam Mahdi, tried to wrest authority from the Maliki scholarly-legal class: the authority to interpret, to transmit, to know, teach, and formulate theology and law. Malikism, however, with its powerful regional tradition already intermeshed at a variety of local levels, would not be easily erased. And after a decade or so of attempted reform and reformulation, the reform effort began to slacken and Malikism would gradually be re-adopted, surviving in this way, and for a second time in Maghribi history, a messianic assault and attempted re-write. As with the (first) Fatimid crisis, it would emerge more resilient, as the main regional tradition of learning, law, and political legitimacy. This indeed is one of the main legacies of 'Iyad, and of the

---

5 For a recent article developing related ideas, see Albarrán Iruela, "From the Islamic West to Cairo."

6 Maribel Fierro, "The Legal Policies of the Almohad Caliphs and Ibn Rushd's Bidayat al-Mujtahid." *Journal of Islamic Studies* 10, no. 3 (1999): 226–48.

Almoravid period more broadly, when the foundations of this religious and intellectual tradition were set, along with the associated state and urban patterns and structures, which would also survive in modified form, as a Far Maghribi state and imperial tradition evolved over the next few centuries.

The Banu Ghaniya Dynasty and Mallorcan Rebellion

While the long-term impact of the empire is perhaps most salient (and what deserves to be underscored here, as the significant regional legacy), the dynasty itself also established a shorter-term legacy, which was not immediately erased by the Almohad onslaught and which is often overlooked. The charisma that attaches itself to ruling families, which so often makes them dangerous claimants during successions and political transitions, attached itself likewise to the descendants of 'Ali b. Yusuf. One branch in particular, that of the Banu Ghaniya, stood out for its resilience, becoming a thorn in the side of the Almohad Empire, which it could never seem to remove, no matter how hard they tried. The Banu Ghaniya rose in prominence bolstered by a connection with the Masufa, a group in the eastern/central Maghrib that became increasingly important after the Almohads had cut off southern trade routes. Yahya b. Ghaniya and his brother Muhammad, were sons of 'Ali b. Yusuf and Ghaniya, a Masufa Almoravid princess. Yahya had been governor of Murcia and Valencia and had defended the provinces for 13 years against Alfonso I of Aragon, *el Batallador*, before being forced to capitulate. As the Almohads consolidated control of the Maghrib, Yahya b. Ghaniya (joined by Yahya b. al-Sahrawiyya) became the centre of Almoravid resistance in southern al-Andalus and the northern Maghrib, holding control of the strait through Ceuta, where 'Iyad and Yahya b. al-Sahrawiyya (who had been governor of Fes) briefly held out. Yahya's brother, Muhammad, had been appointed governor of Mallorca (one of the Balearic Islands) in 520/1126, and family and clan members and other Almoravid loyalists began to flee here when the last Almoravid hold-outs in al-Andalus were defeated (including Yahya b. Ghaniya who died defending Granda in 543/1148.)[7] Muhammad b. Ghaniya's Almoravid kingdom of Mallorca declared itself autonomous and survived from piracy and maritime commerce, the flow and frequency of which was burgeoning as regional players such as Aragon, Pisa, and Genoa (aside from the Maghribi principalities) became more active in Mediterranean trade. Muhammad b. Ghaniya's son, Ishaq, succeeded him in ruling the kingdom, in 551/1156, after a palace shake-up. Ishaq's succession confirmed the stability of the dynasty of the Banu Ghaniya, which enjoyed surprising durability, in spite of its eventful and conflictive history, involving an obstinate war of attrition with the Almohad state.

When Ishaq died during an expeditionary raid in 579/1183, he was succeeded by his older son, Muhammad, who was pressed to recognize Almohad suzerainty; an Almohad emissary would install himself in Mallorca. The population of the island rebelled, however, electing Muhammad's brother, 'Ali, who saw no other option than to take the fight to the Almohads. 'Ali gathered a considerable fleet (32 ships, indication of the kingdom's naval strength), sailed for Bougie and took the city by storm. He then forged alliances with regional Arab Hilali tribes (Riyah, Athbaj, and Judham). 'Ali left his brother Yahya in charge in Bougie and headed west where he took Algiers, Muzaya, and Miliana. When the Almohad Caliph, Ya'qub al-Mansur, became fully apprised of the situation, he sent a major fighting expedition against 'Ali, which was able to retake the lost cities, but not extinguish the rebels. 'Ali and Yahya retreated into the desert, and made for the Jarid in Tunisia where they regrouped, develop new allies, and expanded their zone of activity again, taking Tozeur and Ghafsa and raiding Mahdiyya and Tunis. Al-Mansur sent another large force (of six thousand horsemen) and inflicted a heavy defeat on 'Ali's forces and retook Tozeur and Gafsa. But the rebels persisted. 'Ali and Qaraqush, an Armenian

---

7 Georges Marçais, "Ghāniya," EI2.

chief (and nephew of Salah al-Din) who became a key ally, regrouped and began to raid and campaign once again. 'Ali died in 583/1187, but his chieftaincy would pass to his brother, Yahya, who persisted doggedly, inflicting worse damage than his brother had, at one point taking Tripoli, Mahdiyya, Biskra, Tébessa, Qayrawan, Bone, and Tunis, after the Almohad governor surrendered in 600/1203. Another Almohad expedition was launched, again forcing Yahya to retreat after suffering another defeat on the Tajura plain. The Almohad Caliph al-Nasir then installed Abu Muhammad b. Abi Hafs as governor of Tunis (which would create an important, first autonomous, then post-Almohad dynasty, that of the Hafsids), and Yahya retreated to the Central Maghrib and then west to Sijilmasa after spending some time in Waddan. He died in 633/1237 "harrying and pilaging," after almost fifty years of activity, and by which time the Almohad Empire had broken up into successor states.[8]

* * *

Dynasties are not synonymous with empires, however. And although the story of the clan at the heart of the Almoravid Empire (and its surprisingly long-lived Banu Ghaniya sidekick) was central to the cohesion of the leadership, the social and cultural history of the Almoravid Maghrib transcends the history of both of these clans. The social, political, and religious movement involved in the creation of the Almoravid state left a very different looking Maghrib from what was there before. It had been transformed on multiple levels: Commercial contacts and trade routes connected the region across the Sahara, the Mediterranean, and Eastern North Africa, connecting towns and markets in the region, both to their hinterlands and to the wider world around. A new state and fiscal system, on an entirely new scale and centred in the western Maghrib, had appeared and would be inherited by the successor empires and states of the Western Maghrib. A

---

8 For more on the career of Yahya b. Ghaniya see Baadj, *Saladin, the Almohads and the Banū Ghāniya*, 154–73.

literate class, also on a new scale, had emerged, which was instrumental to the administration, education, and religious life of the new state and would be crucial to the communication and commerce with that wider Muslim world, as the Far Maghrib became a new regional force and player in religion, politics, and culture. None of this is to say that the Almoravids introduced uncontested unity into the region, that this unity would not be disrupted or disputed, or that this unity was unremittingly or objectively positive for the actors and communities involved. Rather, it is to point out that a new set of social, economic, and political structures, with clear counterparts in religion and culture, had appeared in the region as agents of change and that these would have to be dealt with by later generations: building on them, contesting, accommodating, co-opting, and re-inscribing. The vestiges and traces of this past can be discerned in the region's more recent past and even in its present, where they echo and shimmer like a ghost.

Figure 11: Al-Murabitin Elementary School: a primary school outside Taroudant, the capital of the Sus Valley. Photograph by Camilo Gómez-Rivas.

Conclusion

From the perspective of the Maghrib, the Almoravid empire was pivotal and foundational, ushered in by a period of indigenous state formation on a new scale. The foregoing discussion has aimed at unpacking the details, dimensions, and aspects of this transformation, underscoring the fact that it went far beyond mere religious development, and that its roots and causes were likewise not merely religious or ideological, but an interaction with the wider economic, social, and political context was at work. The success of Almoravid trade and diplomatic and commercial recognition by their neighbours was central to their development. The beginning of the integration of Andalusi exiles into Maghribi governing and administrative circles was also an important factor. The broad military and economic exchange taking place along the Andalusi Muslim–Christian frontier was also a powerful economic and social mobilizer. It bears repeating and underscoring that the argument put forth in this book has not aimed to single out the Almoravid leadership as the sole most important factor in causing the various transformations discussed. They are but the most prominent agents in a historiographical record shaped precisely to ascribe such responsibility. Several factors and forces came together to allow for a transformation that no amount of political will could have generated and that no top-down scheme could have implemented. This book has aimed, rather, to point to the multiple dimensions and factors involved in bringing about the social, political, and religious transformation of the Far Maghrib that coincided with the Almoravids.

This richer perspective had been lost to much previous scholarship, and English-language scholarship especially. My own emphasis has been in two areas: One related to what can be perceived about the institutional growth of the Far Maghrib through the development of the legal network and of the texts this network produced. This would grow much more powerful in terms of influence and quantity in later centuries. Moroccan Malikism would come to play a leading role in the region; but it was founded in the Almoravid period, and, as a comprehensive legal-ethical literary tradition, it comprised and engaged many levels of society and activity, from money exchange and sales contracts to the shape of advanced literacy education and ritual expression and identification. A second dimension I have emphasized is related, to a certain extent, to the previous point: While Far Maghribi Malikism (like Far Maghribi historical writing) is, in some ways, much like that of its neighbours (the Almoravids didn't "invent" either of these traditions); what ended up being produced involved a subtle but important shift in perspective. Works that stem from neighbouring traditions, such as 'Abd Allah b. Buluggin's first person history or even Qadi 'Iyad's *Tartīb al-Madārik*, display the shift in perspective brought about by the shift in political and cultural power. There isn't something dramatically Almoravid about these works, and certainly not particularly Berber either. Yet they betray this highly significant change in perspective, in which elite literate production starts to take shape in a place that had not had high traditions of literature, government, historiography, and law. These were borrowed and co-opted traditions, adapted and absorbed in a first generation under the Almoravids, and more profoundly transformed and adapted in later generations.

Much of the emphasis has been interpretive, by reading texts and paying greater attention to the context of their composition and audience and not just their formal elements, by which measure they may closely resemble the neighbouring traditions. This interpretive effort is especially necessary because of the thinness of the record itself. The Almoravid Maghrib likely had a thriving Berber language culture, which was almost certainly transformed in our period, but in a way at which we can only guess. The archaeological record is also scant, but potentially promising. Much remains to be excavated, restored, and studied. Nevertheless, without the important archaeological work of the last few decades, which has shone light on the demographic and economic changes of the Almoravid Maghrib, this work would not have been written. And it is likely archaeology and the study of material culture, which will shed the most new light on this exciting period. Although, it's not as if the textual record were fully known and threadbare. There is a wealth of texts that have neither been edited nor read widely enough. It is my hope that the richness of the picture painted here encourages more sustained investigation into what remains a neglected but exciting field.

Time Line

Pilgrimage of Yahya b. Ibrahim	427/1036
Death of Yahya b. Ibrahim and Guddala revolt against Ibn Yasin	ca. 444/1053
Beginning of Almoravid jihad under Lamtuna	later 440s/1050s
Conquest of Awdaghust and Sijilmasa	446/1054–55
Capture of Aghmat	450/1058
Death of Ibn Yasin	451/1059
Succession of Abu Bakr b. ʿUmar	451/1059
Abu Bakr's marriage to Zaynab al-Nafzawiyya	460/1068
Foundation of Marrakesh	ca. 462/1070
Abu Bakr returns south and Yusuf b. Tashfin becomes amir	463/1071
Conquest of Fes	467/1074-5
Conquest of Tangier and Ceuta	477/1084
Fall of Toledo	478/1085
Yusuf b. Tashfin's first incursion in al-Andalus	479/1086
Battle of Zallaqa	479/1086
Yusuf b. Tashfin conquers al-Andalus	480–483/1088–1091

Succession of 'Ali b. Yusuf	500/1106
Muhammad b. Tumart banished from Marrakesh by 'Ali b. Yusuf	514/1121
Death of 'Ali b. Yusuf	537/1142
Fall of Marrakesh	542/1147
Qadi 'Iyad leads defence of Ceuta against Almohad armies	543/1148
Banu Ghaniya activity against Almohads	543–633/1148–1237

Glossary of Key Terms

[ignoring the initial "al-"]

'Abbasids	Second and greatest dynasty of caliphs of classical Islam, based in Baghdad.
agadir (*agadīr*)	Fortified granary. From Tashelhit.
Almohads	Arabic *al-Muwaḥḥidūn*, from *waḥda*, unity or oneness. Masmuda Berber dynasty that ruled the Maghrib and al-Andalus immediately after the Almoravids.
'amal ahl al-Madīna	Maliki legal concept concerning the normative value of the practice of the Prophet's community at Medina and as preserved by ensuing generations there.
Amazigh	Berber language and people.
Ayyubids	Kurdish dynasty that conquered Egypt and Syria from the Fatimids.
amir (*amīr*)	Commander.
Amīr al-Mu'minīn	Commander of the Believers, classical caliphal title used by the earliest Caliphs (as well as by Almohad Caliphs).
Amīr al-Muslimīn	Commander of the Muslims, new title adopted by the Almoravid amirs.
al-Andalus	Muslim Iberia.

Atlas Mountains	Major mountain chain of Morocco, includes High, Middle and Anti Atlas.
Bajaliyya Shi'a	Little-known early Shi'i community in the Sus Valley.
Barghawata	Early Muslim community from Atlantic plain of Morocco with heterodox beliefs and practices, including (and reportedly) separate revelation and prophet.
Berber	Indigenous people and languages of North Africa, from the Siwa Oasis to the Atlantic. Modern movements adopted Amazigh as umbrella identifier for a diverse group of communities, cultures, and languages.
biographical dictionary (*ṭabaqāt, tarājim*)	Major Arab-Islamic classical textual genre, identifying key individuals, genealogies, and networks within important fields and locations (e.g., teachers and students of a legal school, notables of a city, Sufis, poets).
burnous (*burnus*)	Loose hooded cloak.
caliphate	Classical Islamic institution of leadership based on concept of succeeding the Prophet as leader of the universal Islamic community.
congregational mosque	Main mosque of a city, serving important administrative, legal, and educational functions.
dīnār	Gold coin.
dirham	Silver coin.
dīwān (pl. *dawāwīn*)	Administrative office of government.
Fatimids	Most important Isma'ili Shi'i empire of medieval period, originating in Ifriqiya. Established capital in Cairo.
fatwā	Non-binding but authoritative opinion given by a jurisconsult (mufti).
Gazula	The Saharan tribe of 'Abd Allah b. Yasin, often considered part of the Sanhaja confederation.

geniza	Cache of documents preserved in a synagogue. Most famous one found in Mosque of Ben Ezra in Fustat-Cairo.
al-Gharb al-Islami	Western lands of Islamic World: Iberia, the Maghrib, West Africa.
Guddala	The Berber Saharan Sanhaja tribe of Ibn Yasin's first mission, part of the Almoravid confederation, but who rebelled and had to be repeatedly pacified.
ḥadīth	Words and actions of Prophet Muhammad as preserved by companions and transmitted to later generations. Important source of law. Words and actions of associated individuals can also form part of this corpus.
hajj	Pilgrimage to Mecca, incumbent on individuals possessing the ability. One of the five pillars of Islam.
Hashim	Banu Hashim was the clan of Muhammad, a clan of the Quraysh of Mecca, caretakers of the Ka'aba at time of the revelation.
Ibadi	One of the main branches of Kharijism with contemporary communities in 'Uman, East Africa, southern Algeria, and northeastern Libya.
'idda	Period of time observed before marriage or remarriage lawful.
Ifrani	Related to Banu Ifran, a Zanata Berber tribe.
imām	Leader of a Muslim community, alternately meaning leader of prayer, spiritual leader of a community, religious or religiously-inflected political leader of a community, and in Shi'isim, a divinely designated descendant of Muhammad and leader of the universal community of Muslims.
Isma'ili	Sevener Shi'i Muslim communities with widespread distribution in medieval and modern periods.

jinn	Non-human, invisible and intelligent beings that inhabit a variety of spaces including less populated ones and who vary in nature and intention.
Kharijites (sing. *Khārijī*, plural *Khawārij*)	One of earliest articulated Muslim theological stances, identifying a sectarian community, later characterized as heterodox. Membership in the community of believers, the effect of sin, and the nature of leadership were key focal elements.
Lamtuna	Berber Saharan Sanhaja tribe Ibn Yasin joined after relation with the Guddala soured. The Lamtuna chief Yahya b. 'Umar became Ibn Yasin's patron, forming the core of the Almoravid movement.
madhhab (pl. *madhāhib*)	Sunni Schools of law, which can be characterized more expansively as ethical and higher learning traditions of broad social and political consequence.
madrasa	Higher education institution in the Islamic world, for studies such as law, originating in the fourth/tenth century.
Maghrawa	Berber Zanata and Khariji tribe that controlled Sijilmasa before Almoravids.
Maghrib	Arabic term for North Africa, west of Egypt, sometimes also excluding Tunisia and Libya, and north of Sahara or Sahel.
mahdi	Messianic redeemer figure in Islamic narrative and theological position, existing in both Sunni and Shi'i thought but more central in the latter. Most often described as a descendant of Muhammad returning out of hiding to lead a divinely guided return to justice, although many varieties exist.
Malikism	One of the four principal Sunni *madhhab*s, dominant in al-Andalus, the Maghrib, and West Africa.

marvedí	Spanish term derived from gold dinar currency introduced by Almoravids that gained wide and long-lasting distribution. The term entered several other languages.
Masmuda	Major Berber tribe of the High Atlas and Sus valley that formed basis of Almohad confederation.
Midrarids	Miknasa Berber Khariji tribe that founded Sijilmasa.
miḥrab	Prayer niche directed toward Mecca and focal point in a mosque.
minbar	Stepped pulpit from which an imam delivers a sermon during Friday prayer at the mosque.
Nafzawa	Berber Khariji tribe from which Zaynab al-Nafzawiyya's father descended, from Ifriqiya region.
Nul Lamta	Former caravan town on or close to Atlantic coast in southern Morocco on northwestern point of Saharan trade.
parias	Protection or tribute money paid by individual Ta'ifa kingdoms to Christian kingdoms of northern Iberia, notably Castile–Leon and Aragon.
qāḍī	Judge presiding over an Islamic court.
qaṣr	Castle or fortress; main military administrative building.
Qur'an	The revelation of God through the angel Gabriel to Muhammad, preserved in a single text. The most important and epistemologically most certain source for Islamic knowledge (including as a source of law and faith) in Islam.

Qur'anic taxes	Moneys lawfully paid by individual Muslims on the basis Qur'anic description, such as the zakat or *khums* and as compared to a series of other moneys and taxes levied on individuals and communities which do not appear directly in the Qur'an (and presumably were not Arabian practices), such as the *kharāj*.
ribāṭ	Religious settlement; simple fortification dedicated to the defence and propagation of Islam on its frontier.
Rustumids	Ibadi dynasty based in Tahart, Algeria.
Sahel	Plains region immediately south of the Sahara.
Sanhaja	Major Berber tribal group with Saharan and central Maghribi branches.
Seljuks	First great Islamic Turkic state appearing in the region of Syria and Iraq in the fifth/eleventh century.
Sepharad	Hebrew term for Iberia or Spain.
Shari'a	Islamic law, especially in the sense of the pursuit of True Path as expressed by the Qur'an and the example of Muhammad, in both its strictly legal terms and its moral and ethical dimension.
Shi'a	Smaller of the two most significant faith communities of Islam, largely defined by a belief in the communal mourning of Husayn, the significance of divinely guided imams, and the expectations of the return of the Mahdi.
sīra	Narrative, biographical or hagiographical genre of the life of Muhammad (as compared to non-narrative hadith genre).
Soninke Kingdom of Ghana	West African kingdom encountered by early Almoravid movement, south of the Sahara.
Sudan	Arabic term for region and people south of the Sahara.

Sufism	Popular spiritual movement in Islam that grows dramatically from fifth/eleventh century becoming perhaps the chief spiritual expression of Islam in the post-classical period and involving a variety of practices, social groupings, and theological articulations, yoking asceticism, mysticism, and heightened spirituality.
Sufri	A Khariji sect or set of communities separate from the Ibadis.
Sultan	Leader of a Muslim community, especially in the period after the eclipsing of the Caliph; a "secular" ruler in the Islamic tradition.
Sunni	Larger of the two most significant faith communities of Islam, broadly defined by a belief in normative model of early Muslim community under its first four rulers and the concept of the consensus of the community.
ṭā'ifa (pl. *ṭawā'if*)	Muslim states (often city-states) that emerged after the collapse of Umayyad Córdoba in the fifth/eleventh century.
al-'Udwa	Arabic Andalusi term for the Maghrib, the "other side" of the Mediterranean.
'ulama' (sing. *'ālim*)	Scholars, textual and literate specialists of the Islamic tradition, mostly shaped by the madrasa tradition, and with a primary focus on Islamic traditions of knowledge and perhaps especially law; they played a key role in bureaucratic function of state administration but also had a rich autonomous life.
Umayyads	First dynastic caliphate of Islam, based in Damascus.
Umma	Concept of the universal Muslim community
zajal	Vernacular poetic form, popular in Taïfa kingdoms.

Zanata	Major Berber group that had been influential in late Umayyad al-Andalus and also formed the base for dynastic power in the Maghrib after the fall of the Almohads through the Marinids and 'Abd al-Wadids.
Zirids	Berber Sanhaja dynasty (of the central Maghribi branch) brought in as a military force in late Umayyad Córdoba that established a Taïfa with its capital at Granada after the Umayyad collapse.

Further Reading

General History and Culture of the Islamic West

Abun-Nasr, Jamil M. *A History of the Maghrib in the Islamic Period*. Cambridge: Cambridge University Press, 1987.

Boone, J. L., and N. L. Benco. "Islamic Settlement in North Africa and the Iberian Peninsula." *Annual Review of Anthropology* 28 (1999): 51–71.

Brett, Michael, and Elizabeth Fentress. *The Berbers*. Oxford: Blackwell, 1997.

Brett, Michael. *The Fatimid Empire*. Edinburgh: Edinburgh University Press, 2017.

Fierro, Maribel, ed. *The Routledge Handbook of Muslim Iberia*. London: Routledge, 2020.
    Up to date and exhaustive introduction to various facets of al-Andalus.

Lagardère, Vincent. *Les Almoravides jusqu'au règne de Yūsuf b. Tāšfīn (1039–1106)*. Paris: L'Harmattan, 1989.

Souag, Lameen. "Language Contact in Berber." In *The Oxford Handbook of Language Contact*, edited by Anthony P. Grant, 449–66. Oxford: Oxford University Press, 2020.

Almoravid History and Culture

Bennison, Amira, K. *The Almoravid and Almohad Empires*. Edinburgh: Edinburgh University Press, 2016.

> Detailed but accessible history of the period, with chapters on society, economy, religion, and art. A first step for those wishing to learn more.

Bosch Vilá, Jacinto. *Los Almorávides*. With introduction by Emilio Molina López. Granada: Universidad de Granada, 1998.

Gómez-Rivas, Camilo. "Berber Rule and Abbasid Legitimacy: the Almoravids (434/1042–530/1147)." In *The Routledge Handbook of Muslim Iberia*, edited by Maribel Fierro, 89–114. London: Routledge, 2020.

Messier, Ronald A. *The Almoravids and the Meanings of Jihad*. Oxford: Praeger, 2010.

Moraes Farias, Paolo Fernando. "The Almoravids: Some Questions Concerning the Character of the Movement." *Bulletin de l'IFAN—Série B* 29, no. 3–4 (1967): 794–878.

Saharan and Trans-Saharan History and Culture

Austen, Ralph A. *Trans-Saharan Africa in World History*. Oxford: Oxford University Press, 2010.

Berzock, Kathleen Bickford. *Caravans of Gold, Fragments in Time: Art, Culture, and Exchange across Medieval Saharan Africa*. Evanston: Block Museum of Art, Northwestern University, in association with Princeton University Press, 2019.

> Beautifully illustrated book on vibrant material culture.

Bovill, E. W. *The Golden Trade of the Moors: West African Kingdoms in the Fourteenth Century*. Princeton: Wiener, 1995.

Burkhalter, Sheryl L. "Listening for Silences in Almoravid History: Another Reading of 'The Conquest That Never Was'." *History in Africa* 19 (1992): 103–31.

McDougall, E. Ann. "Saharan Peoples and Societies." In *Oxford Research Encyclopedia of African History*. Oxford University Press, 2019. http://dx.doi.org/10.1093/acrefore/9780190277734.013.285.

Ta'ifa History and Culture

Ferhat, Halima. *Sabta des origines au XIVème siècle*. Rabat: Ministère des Affaires Culturelles, 1993.

Robinson, Cynthia. *In Praise of Song: the Making of Courtly Culture in al-Andalus and Provence, 1005–1134 A.D.* Leiden: Brill, 2002.

Minnema, Anthony. *The Last Ṭā'ifa: The Banū Hūd and the Struggle for Andalusi Political Legitimacy*. Ithaca: Cornell University Press, 2023.
On the political culture of the Ta'ifas.

Religion, Law, and Institutions in Medieval Maghrib and al-Andalus

Albarrán Iruela, Javier. "From the Islamic West to Cairo: Malikism, Ibn Tūmart, al-Ghazā'ī and al-Qāḍī 'Iyāḍ's Death." In *Artistic and Cultural Dialogue in the Late Medieval Mediterranean*, edited by María Marcos Cobaleda, 3–29. Cham: Palgrave MacMillan, 2021.

———. *Veneración y polémica: Muḥammad en la obra del Qāḍī 'Iyāḍ*. Madrid: La Ergástula, 2015.

Casewit, Yousef. *The Mystics of al-Andalus: Ibn Barrajān and Islamic thought in the Twelfth Century*. Cambridge: Cambridge University Press, 2017.

Cornell, Vincent J. *Realm of the Saint: Power and Authority in Moroccan Sufism*. Austin: University of Texas Press, 1998.

El Hour, Rachid. *La Administración Judicial Almorávide en al-Andalus: Élites, negociaciones y enfrentamientos*. Vaajakoski: Academia Scientarum Fennica, 2006.

———. "The Andalusian Qadi in the Almoravid Period: Political and Judicial Authority." *Studia Islamica* 90 (2000): 67–83.

Fierro, Maribel. "Scholars, Jurists and the Legal System," In *The Routledge Handbook of Muslim Iberia*, edited by Maribel Fierro, 290–317. London: Routledge, 2020.

Gómez-Rivas, Camilo. *Law and the Islamization of Morocco under the Almoravids: The Fatwās of Ibn Rushd al-Jadd to the Far Maghrib*. Leiden: Brill, 2014.

Jones, Linda G. *The Power of Oratory in the Medieval Muslim World*. New York: Cambridge University Press, 2012.

Meier, Fritz. "Almoravids and Marabouts." In Fritz Meier, *Essays on Islamic Piety and Mysticism*, 335–421. Leiden: Brill, 1999.

Serrano, Delfina. "Legal Practice in an Andalusī-Maghribī Source from the Twelfth Century CE: The Madhāhib al-ḥukkām fī nawāzil al-aḥkām." *Islamic Law and Society* 7, no. 2 (2000): 187–234.

——. "¿Por qué llamaron los Almohades antropomorfistas a los Almorávides?" In *Los Almohades: problemas y perspectivas*, edited by Maribel Fierro, Patrice Cressier, and Luis Molina, 2:815–47. 2 vols. Madrid: Consejo Superior de Investigaciones Científicas, 2005.

Almohads and the Banu Ghaniya

Baadj, Amar S. *Saladin, the Almohads and the Banū Ghāniya: The Contest for North Africa (12th and 13th Centuries)*. Leiden: Brill, 2015.

Balbale, Abigail Krasner. *The Wolf King: Ibn Mardanish and the Construction of Power in al-Andalus*. Cornell University Press, 2023.
> On power and representation in al-Andalus in the aftermath of Almoravid collapse.

Cressier, Patrice, Maribel Fierro, and Luis Molina, eds. *Los Almohades: problemas y perspectivas*. 2 vols. Madrid: Consejo Superior de Investigaciones Científicas, 2005.

Art, Architecture, and Literature

Bloom, Jonathan. *The Minbar from the Kutubiyya Mosque*. New York / Madrid [Rabat]: Metropolitan Museum of Art / El Viso, Ministry of Cultural Affairs, Kingdom of Morocco, 1998.

Ibn Quzmān, Muḥammad ibn 'Abd al-Malik. *The Mischievous Muse: Extant Poetry and Prose by Ibn Quzmān of Córdoba (d. AH 555/AD 1160)*. Introduction and translation by James T. Monroe. Leiden: Brill, 2017.

Marcos Cobaleda, María. *Los Almorávides: arquitectura de un imperio*. Granada: Universidad de Granada, 2015.

Monroe, James T. "Hispano-Arabic Poetry during the Almoravid Period: Theory and Practice." *Viator* 4 (1973): 65–98.

Stockstill, Abbey. "A Tale of Two Mosques: Marrakesh's Masjid al-Jami' al-Kutubiyya." *Muqarnas Online* 35, no. 1 (2018): 65–82.

Primary Sources in Translation

Anon. *Al-Ḥulal al-Mawšiyya: Crónica árabe de las dinastías almorávide, almohade y benimerín*. Translated by Ambrosio Huici Miranda. Tetouan: Marroquí, 1952.
> Fourteenth century Granadan chronicle variously attributed to Ibn Simāk and Ibn al-Khaṭīb.

al-Bakrī, Abū 'Ubayd. *L'Afrique Septentrionale*. Translated by Mac Guckin De Slane. Paris: Maisonneuve, 1965.

Constable, Olivia Remie. *Medieval Iberia: Readings from Christian, Muslim, and Jewish Sources*. Philadelphia: University of Pennsylvania Press, 1997.
> Standout collection of primary source readings from Arabic, Hebrew, Latin, Castilian, and Catalan.

Corpus of Early Arabic Sources for West African History. Edited by N. Levtzion and J. F. P. Hopkins. Princeton: Wiener, 2000.
> Wonderful collection of Arabic primary source readings on early Islamic West African history.

Ibn 'Abdūn. *Séville Musulmane au début du XIIe siècle: Le traité d'Ibn 'Abdun traduit avec une introduction et des notes par É. Lévi-Provençal*. Paris: Maisonneuve, 1947.

Ibn Buluggīn, 'Abd Allāh. *The Tibyan: Memoirs of 'Abd Allah B. Buluggin, Last Zirid Amir Of Granada*. Translated by Amin T. Tibi. Leiden: Brill, 1986.

Ibn Khaldūn. *Histoire des Berbères et des dynasties musulmanes de l'Afrique Septentrionale*. 4 vols. Paris: Geuthner, 1925.

Ibn 'Idhārī. *al-Bayān al-Mughrib fī Akhbār al-Andalus wa'l-Maghrib*. Edited by E. Lévi-Provençal, G. S. Colin and I. 'Abbā s. 4 vols. Beirut: Dār al-Thaqāfa, 1983.

Mālik b. Anas. *al-Muwaṭṭa', The Royal Moroccan Edition: The Recension of Yaḥyā Ibn Yaḥyā al-Laythī*. Cambridge, MA: Harvard University Press, 2019.

Muḥammad b. 'Iyāḍ. *Madhāhib al-ḥukkām fī nawāzil al-aḥkām (La actuación de los jueces en los procesos judiciales)*. Translated by Delfina Serrano. Madrid: Consejo Superior de Investigaciones Científicas, 1998.

Printed and bound by CPI Group (UK) Ltd, Croydon, CR0 4YY

13/04/2025

14656454-0001